THE AF

"To read Brandon Shimoda's *The Afterlife Is Letting Go* is to be immersed in the afterlife of Japanese American incarceration, which is to say in its ongoing event. In a series of essays, Shimoda explores the ways that the event and sites of incarceration are remembered, memorialized, forgotten, abandoned and altered.

This is a book about incarceration and what it produced, about the textures of memory, haunting, silence, duration and the elasticity of time, and about how places, events and people, remembered and forgotten, marked and unmarked, live on and are held and reanimated in the present. Shimoda shows us again and again what lives on, and how and where. And, drawing together a range of responses to questions about ancestors, camp sites, and the textures of living in the afterlife of violence, Shimoda organizes them into poem, narrative, and inventory.

Both personal and choral, *The Afterlife Is Letting Go* is deeply felt, precise, and as generous in its insights as it is unsparing in its critiques of how 'exclusion zones' proliferate and reach across time and space. A stirring, trenchant, and necessary work."

—**Christina Sharpe**, author of *Ordinary Notes*

"Poet and essayist Brandon Shimoda reconstructs an ever-shifting narration, an unforgettable constellation of voices of the Japanese American incarceration survivors and their children, grandchildren, great grandchildren, including his own. Like the 'hinotama: balls of light' witnessed by the incarcerated *The Afterlife Is Letting Go* also sparks of grief—it's a mourning star, orbiting our collective consciousness of night."

—**Don Mee Choi**, author of *Mirror Nation*

"Brandon Shimoda is investigating ghosts of our ancestors' pasts, for the same reason that I do: to tell their truths, to preserve history on their terms, to put the reader in both his and their shoes. It's done through a poetic, human lens that centers us in a real and honest way, rather than centering how the white gaze might seek to slant the perspective of what happened to us, or worse, to erase the memory of it."

—**Elizabeth Ito**, creator of "City of Ghosts"

"*The Afterlife Is Letting Go* is a powerful exploration of the landscape of mass incarceration that is on the verge of disappearing into the void of forgetting. Using the tactics Shimoda has honed as a poet, he prises open the language of erasure, and in forensic detail traces the disturbing compulsion to deny and suppress, whether through clichés that numb feelings of outrage or proclamations of white guilt that marginalize descendants' efforts to apprehend the scale of destruction that continues to unravel across generations.

As a deeply political text, Shimoda connects the use of Executive Order 9066 in the 1940s to today's carceral structures of racial segregation and culture of fear and hate. Like a detective in a crime novel, he meticulously unearths the remnants of memory in sites scattered across the United States in small towns, cities, deserts, archival records, personal letters, media stories and his own family's lives. Sensitive to the cadences, tonalities and lines of movement in not only words but also places, he gives these remnants the significance they have been denied as witnesses to the truths that question the world as we know it. And as a deeply ethical text, he brings together the work of other Japanese American artists, writers and activists to create a potent archive for those seeking strategies, resources and the courage for the journey into what Shimoda reveals as the afterlife where both the past and future are intrinsically intertwined."

—**Kirsten Emiko McAllister**, author of *Terrain of Memory: A Japanese Canadian Memorial Project*

THE AFTERLIFE
IS LETTING GO

BRANDON
SHIMODA

CITY LIGHTS BOOKS / SAN FRANCISCO

Cover photograph by Midori Shimoda
Cover design by Jeff Mellin
Text design by Patrick Barber

Library of Congress Cataloging-in-Publication Data

Names: Shimoda, Brandon, author.
Title: The afterlife is letting go / Brandon Shimoda.
Description: San Francisco, CA : City Lights Books, 2024.
Identifiers: LCCN 2024018561 (print) | LCCN 2024018562 (ebook) |
    ISBN 9780872869295 (paperback) | ISBN 9780872869301 (epub)
Subjects: LCSH: Japanese Americans. | Shimoda, Brandon—Family.
    | Japanese Americans—Forced removal and internment,
    1942–1945—Influence. | Collective memory—United States. |
    World War, 1939–1945—Japanese Americans. | World War,
    1939–1945—Concentration camps—United States—Influence.
Classification: LCC E184.J3 S463 2024 (print) | LCC E184.J3 (ebook) |
    DDC 940.53/1773089956--dc23/eng/20240425
LC record available at https://lccn.loc.gov/2024018561
LC ebook record available at https://lccn.loc.gov/2024018562

City Lights Books are published at the City Lights Bookstore
261 Columbus Avenue, San Francisco, CA 94133
citylights.com

I remember having this feeling growing up that I was haunted by something, that I was living within a family full of ghosts. There was this place that they knew about. I had never been there, yet I had a memory for it.

REA TAJIRI
History and Memory: for Akiko and Takashige

I think that's why I write: for the hard skull that stubbornly remains, the soft stuff inside that disintegrates, for lost voices, a gossamer touch. I am asking, "Do you remember? Do you care?"

WAKAKO YAMAUCHI
Songs My Mother Taught Me

Or perhaps the contemplation of the past and its memory is the work of the written book, and the realization of being at locations of incarceration finally visceral and unwritable.

KAREN TEI YAMASHITA
KonMarimasu

CONTENTS

How do we memorialize an event that is still ongoing?

CHRISTINA SHARPE
In the Wake: On Blackness and Being

PAPER FLOWERS

ONE EVENING, MANY YEARS AGO, BUT NOT SO MANY years ago, a Japanese man, out for a walk in the American desert, saw a "rare and unusual flower" on the far side of a barbed wire fence, and, leaning closer to look at the flower, was shot in the heart.[1]

The Japanese man had lived in the United States for forty years, but was not a citizen, because he was born in Japan (Takahama, Ishikawa[2]), and Asians could not, at the time of the man's murder, become citizens of the United States. He was one of 8,130 Japanese immigrants and Japanese Americans incarcerated in Topaz, a concentration camp in the Sevier Desert of west-central Utah, and one of the more than 125,000 who were incarcerated in prisons and camps throughout the US.[3] It was April 11, 1943, seven months since the camp opened (September 11).

---

1. Julie Otsuka, *When The Emperor Was Divine* (New York: Anchor, 2003)
2. present-day Shika
3. The Ireicho, the Sacred Book of Names, lists 125,284 persons of Japanese ancestry who were incarcerated in US Army, Department of Justice, Wartime Civil Control Administration, and War Relocation Authority camps, although the number keeps changing as people who were forgotten are remembered.

James Hatsuaki Wakasa, 63, was alone. He had no family. He had dinner with a friend in the mess hall that night—the stoves, dark brown with rust, are still there—then went for a walk along the southwestern edge of camp. The fence, four strands of barbed wire held up with tree limbs, is still there. Later, the friend he had dinner with (Karl Akiya) visited the site and saw, on the far side of the fence, an "unusual flower."[4] He speculated that Wakasa was reaching through the fence to pick the flower when he was shot. That is one of many stories. Another story is that Wakasa was walking his dog. Another is that he was running after the dog. Another is that the dog got caught in the fence. Another is that the dog was not his, but a stray. Another is that he was collecting stones. In her memoir, *Desert Exile*, Yoshiko Uchida writes that Wakasa was looking for "arrowheads, trilobites, or unusual stones." In her YA novel *Journey to Topaz*—a fictionalization of *Desert Exile*—Uchida writes that Wakasa was "reaching for an interesting stone." "Many of the children were told that Wakasa was looking for a flower or a fossil," said TT Takemoto, in an interview about their film *Warning Shot* (2016), which takes a *Rashomon*-like approach to telling the story of Wakasa's murder.[5] The camp newspaper, the *Topaz Times*, reported that Wakasa was crawling under the fence to escape, "and because he was an elderly man he didn't know what he was doing," said George Shimamoto, Issei.[6] In her memoir, *I Call To Remembrance*, Toyo Suyemoto writes that "the old man, in the habit of strolling along the fence for exercise, had no intention of escaping." "He

4. Sandra C. Taylor, *Jewel of the Desert: Japanese American Internment at Topaz* (Berkeley, CA: University of California Press, 1993)

5. Jan Christian Bernabe and Laura Kina, "Muscles, Mash Ups and Warning Shots—Queering Japanese American History: An Interview with Tina Takemoto," *Queering Contemporary Asian American Art*, ed. Laura Kina and Jan Christian Bernabe (Seattle: University of Washington Press, 2017), 220-226

6. George Shimamoto, interview with Sandra Taylor, October 5, 1987

couldn't have been trying to escape," writes Kiku Hughes in her graphic novel *Displacement*. "He knew as well as any of us that there's nowhere to go out there." Beyond the fence was desert. Beyond the desert, mountains. Beyond the mountains, a cruel and uninviting country.

The shot that killed Wakasa was fired from three hundred yards away by a white man in a guard tower. Wakasa may or may not have seen the white man, but he knew he was there. The guard may or may not have called out, may or may not have fired a warning shot or shots. Wakasa may or may not have heard the man calling out, the warning shot or shots. That he was deaf is another story. There was wind that evening. The wind is still there.

The shot that killed Wakasa was at least the tenth shot fired by guards at the Japanese Americans in Topaz, which may or may not mean that the first nine shots *missed*. The guard, Gerald Philpott, was a teenager, 19. He claimed that he "hollered" at Wakasa four times, that Wakasa, looking directly at him, "turned and started to climb the fence," so he "fired one shot to frighten" him.[7] With a thirty-caliber rifle. To have shot Wakasa at three hundred yards, Philpott must have been holding him very tightly in his sights. He was court-martialed and tried for manslaughter. A jury of military personnel found him not guilty. He was acquitted anyway. The camp population, withheld from the truth of its own execution, was not made aware of this. "Particulars and facts of the matter were never satisfactorily disclosed to the residents," writes Miné Okubo in her graphic memoir, *Citizen 13660*.

Philpott's charge sheet lists fourteen witnesses: ten military police officers, three War Relocation Authority [WRA] officials, and Tsune Baba, Nisei, and the chairman of the community council. The youngest witness (not listed) was likely Ron Kiino, who was three. He was playing with a

7. Gerald Philpott, court-martial testimony transcript, April 23, 1943

3

friend beneath Guard Tower 8 when he heard shouting above and looked up. Later in life, when people asked what he remembered about camp, Kiino said, "the wind, the sand, the liver, and the shooting."

The variations in the story of Wakasa's murder—which, in the maelstrom of disinformation and the withholding of evidence, began to flow almost immediately—have become part of the story, but, aside from the perverse, parlor game aspect of trying to guess what Wakasa was doing, why does it matter? The variations reproduce what Jackie Wang calls a "guilt-innocence schematization."[8] If Wakasa was trying to escape, he was guilty. If he was looking at a flower— deaf, with dog, etc.—he was innocent. If Philpott thought Wakasa was trying to escape but Wakasa was reaching for a flower, then it was Philpott's misunderstanding that ended Wakasa's life, not Philpott's racism, its endorsement by the camps, and its reinforcement of the racism of white America. "Innocence," Wang writes, "is just code for *non-threatening to white civil society*."[9]

Two Issei men, members of the camp's landscaping crew, found a 2,000-pound stone, gathered smaller stones and a bag of cement, and erected a monument for Wakasa. Where did the stone come from? Did it fall from the sky? The Issei must have summoned it from the void left in the absence of their friend and brother, one ton, the weight of their feeling. The monument was made to console Wakasa's spirit, give it a place to rest, and give to the community a ritual grave. The stone was imbued with the perspective of eternity. That is where it came from: the ancient lake, deep space, eternity. The stone would outlast everyone, would transcend the memory of those who were there, and those who came after, and would see Topaz and its eventual ruin beyond the end. But eternity came quick. The government

---

8. Jackie Wang, *Carceral Capitalism* (Los Angeles: Semiotext(e), 2018)
9. Ibid.

ordered that the monument be destroyed. A few days later, the 2,000-pound stone was gone.

"Stone of mystery, death, / of deep space and reconciliation," writes Claire Kageyama-Ramakrishnan in her poem "Tale of the Black Diamond." When the monument disappeared, it transmigrated into the realm of collective imagination, became legendary. In its absence and irretrievability, the grave was no longer delimited by the fence or Topaz or the desert or Utah. The grave became the United States, the most general and the most specific reminder of why the Japanese Americans were incarcerated and what could happen to them on any given day in or outside of camp. And yet the stone was not absent, it was not irretrievable, because it had not, as it turned out, been destroyed. When the Issei were ordered to destroy the stone, they dug a hole in the ground, and buried it.

Many years later, but not so many years later, a descendant of Topaz, Nancy Ukai, discovered in the National Archives a map, hand-drawn by George Shimamoto, that diagrams the exact location of Wakasa's murder. It shows the fence, a floodlight pole, the guard towers to the north and south of where Wakasa was walking; it records the distance between Philpott and Wakasa as 943 feet, 6 inches; it notes that there was a "mild westerly wind," and that Wakasa was found face up, his body pointed north, legs folded beneath him.[10] "It felt like Shimamoto, by recording every detail and the distance, down to the inch, was treating the loss of life with respect," Ukai said. "It was its own memorial."

Ukai's parents were incarcerated in Topaz. The first time she heard about Wakasa was when she was 10, at the dinner table. Her mother was talking about Topaz when her voice suddenly changed. "They didn't have to kill him!" she

---

10. "Blood Stain on Ground + Branches of Bitterroot (Sagebrush)," Shimamoto wrote on the map.

shouted. Ukai was startled. "I remember thinking, why is she getting so emotional, why is her face getting red?"[11]

She included the map in an essay, "The Demolished Monument," which she published as part of *50 Objects/50 Stories*, a storytelling project she directs.[12] In September 2020, two archeologists, Mary Farrell and Jeffrey Burton, visited Topaz. They brought Shimamoto's map (from Ukai's essay), a 300-foot measuring tape, and a chaining pin. "We were hoping to find maybe a few fragments of concrete," Farrell said. They started from the footings of Guard Tower 8. 943 feet, 6 inches later, they found a stone sticking up, just slightly, from the dirt. "The smooth stone, lying face down, measures about 4 feet long by 1½ feet wide," they wrote in an article for *Discover Nikkei*. "Its thickness is unknown: it rises less than 3 inches above the ground, but is massive and seemingly unmovable."[13]

"What did you feel when you saw it?" Ukai asked Farrell.

"I thought, oh my god, this is it, this is where Mr. Wakasa died, this is where his friends put up a monument, and...I'm sorry, it makes me emotional just to think about."[14]

A meeting was called to discuss what should be done with the stone. Topaz survivors and descendants, archeologists, the National Park Service, and members of the Topaz Museum—fifteen miles from Topaz, in the town of Delta—agreed that it should remain in the ground. I asked one of the archeologists, Koji Lau-Ozawa, why.

"Excavation and removal are by their nature irreversible and destructive acts," he said. "You can't un-ring that bell."

11. Nancy Ukai and Mary Farrell, *Uncovering a 78-year-old Mystery*, October 15, 2021
12. Nancy Ukai, "The Demolished Monument: James Hatsuaki Wakasa and the erasure of memory," 50 Objects/Stories: 50objects.org
13. Jeffrey Burton and Mary M. Farrell, "The Power of Place: James Hatsuaki Wakasa and the Persistence of Memory," *Discover Nikkei*.
14. Ukai and Mary Farrell, *Uncovering a 78-year-old Mystery*, op. cit.

Lau-Ozawa's grandparents and great-grandparents were incarcerated in the Gila River concentration camp, on the Gila River Indian Reservation in Arizona; much of his work is devoted to close reading the site. He reiterated the "oppressive forces" that resulted in the stone being buried, and invoked the Issei's "touch and interaction with the soil and stone," which he felt when he visited. "I was able to stand next to it and lay my hand upon it," he told me.

In July 2021, the Topaz Museum, without informing survivors, descendants, or the Japanese American community, hired a local backhoe company to remove the stone and relocate it to the museum. "Remove" and "relocate" are resonant, triggering words. Present were two videographers, the Senior Officer of the Utah State Historic Preservation Office, those museum board members who lived close enough (i.e., neither of the two Japanese American board members), and the museum's director.

No archeologists were present. A proper excavation might have included setting up a grid, documenting the surface of the soil, screening for artifacts, collecting soil samples, measuring, photographing, cataloguing everything. The stone was dug out with shovels, then pulled with a forklift and chains into the excoriating light of the twenty-first century. Fragments of stone and pieces of concrete—the monument's original base, maybe—broke off. The stone was dragged across the sand, wrapped with a yellow rigging strap, and placed on a piece of carpet on a wooden pallet. The site of Wakasa's murder was left unmarked, the hole in the ground—five feet deep—backfilled with dirt.

That night, the director of the museum, Jane Beckwith, sent out an email. Subject line: "Rock." "Just a quick report on this morning," the email began. "It only took a couple of hours to remove the dirt and pull the stone out of the hole," she wrote, adding that "a small piece flipped off." The last line of the email: "The crack was not a factor."

"I was crying," Ukai said, about the email. "I didn't expect it to have this physical effect on me," as if her mother's emotions from the dinner table a lifetime ago were, in that instant, released.[15] Ukai replied to the email. "I was stunned to learn that you lifted the Wakasa monument this morning. You appear not to understand that the place where a member of our community was murdered, and where that crime was memorialized by camp inmates, was desecrated at the time by the WRA. In a similar way our agency and our ability to be involved has been taken away from us once again."

Satsuki Ina, a writer, filmmaker, activist, and psychotherapist specializing in community trauma, who was born in the Tule Lake concentration camp after her parents were relocated there from Topaz, also replied. "You have robbed us of a precious moment in time. So heartbreaking to know that you would not consider the meaning of such a moment for all of us survivors and descendants to be a part of a powerful healing experience to uncover the painful burden we carry about our family's suffering."

Masako Takahashi, an artist born in Topaz—her father was the editor of the *Topaz Times,* and her mother wrote for it—who runs the Takahashi Foundation, a charitable organization that supports the Japanese American community, replied too. She had offered to fund, through the Foundation, a proper excavation, including a spiritual healing ceremony. The museum declined. In her email, she noted the "special opportunity" that the stone's unearthing had produced, and urged the museum to include Japanese Americans in telling its story. "Why not invite Japanese Americans to communicate about what it's been like to be Japanese American?"

"An opportunity for survivors, descendants and all those in the Topaz and civil rights community to experience a

---

15. Ukai and Farrell, *Uncovering a 78-year-old Mystery,* op. cit.

powerful chance for healing has been lost forever," Ukai continued in her email. "The memory of James Hatsuaki Wakasa deserved better."

Four days later, the director responded. This time her email was co-signed by the museum board. "We understand your concerns and deep feelings," the email began. The description of the removal was more comprehensive, expressed more concern. There were numerous assurances that the removal and relocation were executed professionally and according to the advice of archeologists. The last paragraph of the email began, "Since the rock is safe..."

Safe from what? From whom? Did the museum think that the stone, buried for seventy-eight years, was unsafe, and had finally—dragged, cracked, a small piece flipped off, now exposed—achieved the protection it needed? In August, in a letter to Ina, Takahashi, and Ukai, the director introduced into the story of the stone's removal and relocation a concern that had not, until then, been expressed: that the stone, newly discovered, its coordinates revealed, was in danger of being vandalized or destroyed, and that *that* was the reason why it had to be removed right away. In the letter, the director cited examples of vandalism around Topaz, bullet holes in stop signs, tire tracks running off the road. Other, entirely visible and accessible memorials to Wakasa—a sign mounted on a metal post, a handwritten plaque near the camp's sewage plant, a tree trunk carved IN MEMORY WAKASA—had not been vandalized, so why would a stone, whose location could only be known to readers of *Discover Nikkei* or *50 Objects*, who would then have to measure out—starting where? with what?—943 feet, 6 inches, be at greater risk?

In September 2021, a group of camp survivors and descendants (including Ukai, Ina, Takahashi), filmmakers, and historians, with an advisory council of archeologists, scholars, artists, and Buddhist priests, formed the Wakasa Memorial Committee. They sent a letter to the museum outlining measures to "remedy" the situation, including by conducting an archeological assessment, making public the video of the stone's removal, and apologizing for the desecration of the memorial site. The letter referred to the removal as "crude, reckless," and a violation of the museum's mission, the opening commitment of which is "To preserve the Topaz site and its WWII history."

The same month, the Friends of Topaz, a group formed in 2013 by Topaz descendants as a "direct link between the Topaz Museum and the Topaz community," published a letter defending the museum's actions, citing "the climate of vicious anti-Asian hate" that necessitated the immediate removal of the monument. The climate was—and is—real and relentless, and stretches deep into even Asianless landscapes. "In its haste, however," the letter continued, "the museum failed to notify the community in advance of the removal, thereby triggering anger and leading some to conclude that it acted with callous indifference."[16]

The museum's "haste" was "unconscionable," wrote Karen Korematsu, daughter of Fred Korematsu, who famously refused the exclusion order and fought incarceration all the way to the Supreme Court. "All incarceration sites and Indigenous lands need to be viewed as sacred," she wrote. "Accountability and transparency are the only way to stop multi-generational trauma across all racial communities."[17]

What, in the context and chaos of this history, does it mean to protect a 2,000-pound stone? The WMC and the Topaz Museum each expressed their commitment to the stone's

16. Wakasa monument statement from the Friends of Topaz, September 2, 2021

17. Dr. Karen Korematsu, Foreword, *Show Me the Way to Go to Home* (Santa Fe, NM: Radius Books, 2023)

protection, and found themselves embodying, in their ideas of how to carry out that commitment, a particular ideology—embodying, however reluctantly, a *side*. The museum believed that they were protecting the stone from potential harm. The WMC believed that the museum caused exactly the kind of harm from which it claimed to be protecting it. They could not understand how people in the community could defend the actions of the museum and place the museum's actions above the community's interests. Those who defended the actions of the museum could not understand how the WMC could defame the institution that was preserving their history. Because the museum was giving space to a history that was, in that remote, Asianless place, otherwise likely to be lost, to criticize the museum threatened the already precarious nature of Japanese American memory and amounted to an act of disloyalty—to the museum, and to the community.

A rift runs through the community, always threatening, perennially, to break it. The rift was formed during the war and widened along the question of loyalty—how loyal the Japanese Americans were to the United States, a system to which the community, in allegiance or dissent, was bound. The question was not, of course, how loyal the United States was to the Japanese Americans; that had already been answered. The Japanese Americans being were being forced not only into proving their loyalty—through their movements, behaviors, ways of speaking, associations, and, most formally, through their responses to a loyalty questionnaire[18]—but into a willingness to do so, at whatever

18. In early 1943, all adults were required to fill out a questionnaire that was designed to both recruit Nisei for combat and to assess individual eligibility for early release/resettlement. The final question, and especially the consequences for how it was answered, has been written about extensively, and continues to haunt the community: "Will you swear unqualified allegiance to the United States of America and faithfully

length, and set against the unquestioned, irreproachable loyalty of white Americans. Proving loyalty became an orientation, an identity. Every Japanese American, from those on their deathbed to those born one minute ago, became a symbol of how much and how deeply, or how little, they subscribed and adhered to the kind of conditional, exclusionary Americanism they were being offered—which the collaborationist Japanese American Citizens League [JACL] was zealous to endorse. The community was entrapped in a series of limited viewpoints and positions, in which were implied an ethics of right and wrong—ways to attend to history, to protect and preserve it, to protest and watch over it. Every Japanese American became a flag.

The pinnacle proof of loyalty was achieved in the community policing itself—people accusing each other of being disloyal, to the United States or to the community, to individuals or to the meaning and momentum of their story. The pinnacle was topped by the flag of each person growing accustomed to also policing themselves. It became a tradition, enforced by white supremacy, a system in which white people—friends and neighbors, administrators and monsters, strangers and saints—could, on the periphery, remain silent.

With a 2,000-pound stone wedged—risen—into the rift, the community was, once again, threatened by, and threatening itself with, the question—the crisis—of how best to take care of itself.

But what if internecine struggle is a testing, therefore a renewal, of vows? What if critical differences in opinion are a re-dedication of love?

---

defend the United States from any and all attacks by foreign and domestic forces, and forswear any form of allegiance or disobedience to the Japanese Emperor, or any other foreign government, power, or organization?"

Or, what if the "rift" that threatens to break the community, whether formed from within or enforced from without, is not only what holds it together, but what defines it?

Or, what if, prior to the government's expedient perception and subsequent compressing of many peoples—diverse and incommensurable in origin and orientation, experience and perspective—into a single, containable body, there was no community at all?

At first, the flower was "unusual." Then, through Julie Otsuka, it became "rare." Was it rare and unusual to James Hatsuaki Wakasa, or was it rare and unusual in that desert? Was it rare and unusual for the way it looked, the way it was growing, the way it held the sun, repelled the sun, the wind and dust, for being strange and somewhat impossible?

"No flowers grow / where dust winds blow," writes Janice Mirikitani in her poem "Desert Flowers." The flowers that adorned Wakasa's casket were made of paper. "The women of each block made enormous floral wreaths with paper flowers," writes Miné Okubo in *Citizen 13660*. "They brought crepe paper, scissors, artificial leaves, wires and buckets and worked at the mess hall tables," writes Toyo Suyemoto in *I Call to Remembrance*. The sound of women deep inside a concentration camp folding paper into flowers, the sound of paper flowers blossoming out of women's hands, the sound of paper flowers pressing against the walls, the ceiling, overflowing the windows, eating the dust, conducting and overseeing the sadness, the anguish; the sound of paper flowers being folded—by people together and alone, one at a time or in rainbows—into a new millennium. According to the WRA's report on Wakasa's funeral, the paper flowers "would put to shame an equal display of real flowers." The report reveals, without irony, a greater sympathy for the paper flowers than for the man they were meant to observe, although maybe it was the reporter's way of revealing his sympathy, subliminally. "It seemed a shame that such beauty, which, from its very inanimate, physical nature, should have lived so brief a span."[19]

Two thousand people—one-fourth of the camp's population—attended the funeral. There were prayers, a sermon, benediction, four reverends. Kaoru Inouye sang "Rock of Ages," "cleft for me, let me hide myself in Thee," evoking the image of mourners forming a procession and disappearing into the stone. Wreaths of paper flowers were propped up on tripods beneath a basketball hoop with no net. Wakasa's coffin, wearing the grief of the congregation in the form of paper flowers, was carried by six men. The shadows of the paper flowers draped the coffin with the wavering impression of bowed heads listening. The wind picked up. "The paper flowers rustled and shook."[20] Wakasa's body was driven to Ogden, where it was cremated. Where did his ashes go after that?

"No turning back," writes Brian Komei Dempster in his poem "Crossing." He is driving to Topaz to visit, for the first time, the place where his mother was incarcerated as a child, and is projecting his anticipation onto the landscape.

I rush

past salt beds, squint at the horizon for the desert's
    edge: a lone tower, a flattened barrack, some sign of
    Topaz. [21]

19. Russell A. Bankson, "The Wakasa Incident," War Relocation Authority, Central Utah Project, Topaz, Utah, May 10, 1943
20. Ibid.
21. Brian Komei Dempster, "Crossing," *Topaz* (New York: Four Way Books, 2013)

The moment we turned off Interstate 15 onto Highway 50, it started to rain. I squinted through the windshield looking for shapes on the horizon, even though we were 40 miles from Topaz. The horizon was auspicious, releasing premonitions, like fireworks, into the clouds.

The desert on which Topaz was inscribed was inhabited, for one thousand years, by the Goshute, Southern Paiute, Timpanogos, and Ute peoples. Until the late 1840s–early 1850s, when the Mormons arrived. With them came disease, the death and displacement of the tribes, the steady degradation of the land. Mormons, whose realization of Zion was overseen by an extraterrestrial god, approved the land as sacred, and claimed it for their own. They overfished the rivers and lakes, which they drained anyway to irrigate crops. Mormon cattle ate and depleted plants the tribes relied on for food. Within twenty years, the land had been transformed and the tribes were confined to reservations, which settlers continued to whittle down in size to serve their own, heedless imaginations.

The rain was a membrane. The mountains were mist. A yellow light, the light of dawn in early evening, pushed against the clouds. "Look at that yellow cloud," Koko Tanaka says, in Wakako Yamauchi's play *12-1-A*, when she and her family arrive in Poston. "Like in Kansas maybe. Like in the movies."

As Yumi slept, Lisa and I listened to Kishi Bashi's "In Fantasia," a song we first heard on *The Babysitter's Club*, Season 2, Episode 7, in which Claudia Kishi's grandmother, Mimi Yamamoto, dies. When Claudia (Momona Tamada) lights a stick of incense on the funeral altar next to a framed photograph of Mimi holding a magenta flower, "In Fantasia" fades in, the effervescence of Kishi Bashi's violin like spirits ascending.

In an earlier episode (Season 1, Episode 6), it is revealed that Mimi (Takayo Fischer) was incarcerated as a child in Manzanar.[22] It is the only moment in *The Babysitter's Club* when the narrative breaks from the present to permit history to intervene and inform, maybe even explain, the characters' emotions. A surprising moment, affirming, but also frustrating that the Japanese American characters are the ones in the show to carry the burden of history.

"I had a dream that a giraffe ate a whole grass," Yumi said, waking up. "Then I had a dream that I fell into a pond of dark water."
　　"Did you drown?"
　　"No, I jumped out and landed on a rock."

In the spring of 1942, facing a cruel and sudden—a hasty—deadline, many thousands of Japanese Americans were burdened with the question of what to do with everything they were forced to leave behind: their homes, shops, markets, hotels, and everything in them; their farms and everything on them; their cars and trucks, their pets, the effects of their histories, their material connections to Japan. Those who did not sell or give away or hide or burn or bury their belongings, handed them over, in good faith, to friends and neighbors, who offered to take care of them in their absence. When they returned, many found their homes and businesses ransacked, their farms in ruins, their belongings gone. Others found that their friends and neighbors had kept their word. These friends and neighbors became saints, their names passed down as heirlooms. But the heirlooms came with a price. It came, that is, with a debt.

---

22. Fischer was incarcerated as a child in Rohwer and has appeared in at least three other films about Japanese American incarceration: *Only the Brave* (2006), *Stand Up for Justice: The Ralph Lazo Story* (2004), and *Strawberry Fields* (1997).

I had a theory before visiting the Topaz Museum: that it is not *for* Japanese Americans, but *about* them. And that it might not even be about them.

The seeds of the museum were sown when Delta High School's English teacher turned her students on to the concentration camp off the edge of town. Journalism, early 1980s. Students were given the assignment of interviewing people who had worked at Topaz. "They weren't very good interviewers," their teacher told me. If they did not like what the person said—if, for example, the person referred to the Japanese Americans as "Japs"—her students would end the interview. "Japs," the teacher said, which felt, when she said it, like a nail being driven through my foot, no, my entire body. Students drove out to Topaz, walked the ruins, scavenged artifacts. They were so enthusiastic about drawing the story out of the past, and out of the ground, they "literally ran to class."[23] They could have practiced the "catch and release" method of archeological study by returning everything to where they had found it, but it was not archeological, it was extractive. The act of removing objects from Topaz, lifting them out of the ground, became ritual. The objects were kept, at first, at the teacher's house. A large enough collection was amassed to open a museum, to which survivors and descendants of Topaz began to donate objects and money, once again handing over their belongings, in good faith, to be taken care of in their absence.

The English teacher and the museum director were the same person. One of the sentiments I heard most often from people who defended, whether or not they personally agreed with, the museum's removal and relocation of the stone, was that the museum was providing a place where

23. James Sloan Allen, "A Town, a Teacher and a Wartime Tragedy," *Learning for Justice*, June 16, 2011: learningforjustice.org/magazine/a-town-a-teacher-and-a-wartime-tragedy

the community could preserve the memory of what they endured, and that without it—and without the stalwart efforts of the director, in particular—not only the preservation but the memory of the past would risk endangerment if not extinction. The sentiment seemed to be that one infraction, however significant, should not undermine the museum's more enduring work.

People outside the community, however—white people who had little to do with the community—offered paeans to the museum and its director that did little to hide the disdain they felt for the Japanese Americans. "This wonderful museum would not exist, if not for the monumental efforts of Jane Beckwith," wrote Delta resident and Topaz Museum docent Beverly DeWyze in a letter to the *Millard County Chronicle Progress* expressing "dismay" over the criticism she received after removing the stone. "Hundreds of others have contributed work, money, inspiration, and suggestions," she wrote, "but there would have been nothing to contribute to without her."[24] As if all of the work, money, inspiration, and suggestions would otherwise be sucked, in the absence of altruistic ingenuity, into the vacuum created by a Japanese American lack of memorial will. James Sloan Allen, political scientist, likewise wrote: "But the Topaz camp itself might have remained only a subject for historians and a painful memory for Japanese Americans, while likely vanishing from its forlorn desert site beside a lonely historic marker, had it not been for a high school teacher in Delta named Jane Beckwith."[25] As if without the director's humanitarianism, the Japanese Americans would have no recourse to memory, might not have any memory at all.

24. Beverly DeWyze, "Letter to the Editor: On the Wakasa Memorial," *Millard County Chronicle Progress*, December 22, 2021
25. James Sloan Allen, "A Town, a Teacher and a Wartime Tragedy," *Learning For Justice*

The people I knew who visited Topaz offered praiseworthy yet more down-to-earth portraits of the director: that she was their host, their guide; drove them to and from Topaz in her truck ("an old stick shift. The door won't really open," writes Kimiko Tanabe, whose grandmother Miyeko was incarcerated in Topaz, in her journal); invited them to her house; was endlessly knowledgeable and enthusiastic and generous; that she went out of her way.

The director, as it turned out, did and was all of these things. She opened the museum for us; it was Sunday, the museum was closed. When we arrived, she was in the lobby, vacuuming a couch. She did not see us, the door was locked, so we watched her through the glass. "This is her house," I thought. When she let us in, she welcomed us as if she knew us. When she ushered us through the museum, she pointed out things that were meaningful to her, making sure we did not miss anything, and was solicitous, asking us what we thought about the installations, the artifacts, how things were arranged, what should be done with various objects and works of art still in storage, as if the museum was a work-in-progress, our opinion was important, we were there to help her complete it.

The museum is an "introductory" museum, she explained. Most of its visitors—10,000 per year—are white, she told me, and know little to nothing about the history. Many of them, she also told me, have never seen a Japanese or Japanese American person before, which I found impossible to believe. ("There is a Japanese American family in Gunnison," she said. Ninety miles away.) If true, it meant that their introduction to Japanese Americans was, in this benighted, retrogressive twenty-first century, as specimens in a museum.

Past the lobby, before the main exhibition, was a gallery with glass display cases, illuminated, set into the walls. They held objects, jewelry and figurines mostly, made from tiny shells. They looked confectionary. There was such an abundance of shell art that it might have seemed, to the visitor who knew little to nothing about the history, that the main avocation in camp was collecting shells and transforming them, meticulously, into bouquets. "Instead of huddling in their barracks, whining for three years," wrote DeWyze, in that same letter to the local paper, "they created beautiful things."[26]

The archetypal orientation towards Japanese people was laid bare in that sentence: praise the art, put down the people. But also, what would it have mattered—to that Delta resident, to anyone—if the people behind barbed wire spent three years "huddling in their barracks, whining"? Is there a *right* way to be incarcerated? As I peered through the glass, I perceived the jewelry and figurines as evidence that the Japanese Americans were exacting, in miniature, an alternate universe.

The art made in camp and the exhibitions that have brought the art to light express to me not only ingenuity—the art is always breathtaking yet humble, precise yet unpretentious—but a representation of one of the central conditions of incarceration: time. Crawling, indefinite time. The art embodies what Nicole Fleetwood calls, in *Marking Time: Art in the Age of Mass Incarceration*, a "carceral aesthetics—the production of art under the conditions of unfreedom," which involves "the creative use of penal space, time, and matter." Most exhibitions have centered a triumphalist narrative, of the individual and their ability to overcome the conditions of their incarceration. But one does not overcome so much as they are dragged across the hallucination that is crawling, indefinite time. As Jane Dusselier writes, in *Artifacts of Loss: Crafting Survival in Japanese American Concentration Camps*, "a forced

26. DeWyze, "Letter to the Editor: On the Wakasa Memorial"

leisure interpretation of camp-made art is problematic because it suggests that internal artwork is evidence of humane treatment." In representations of camp life, and in the frame of these artworks, the administration is generally absent. That, along with the triumphalist narrative, which envisions the survivor emerging whole, and made whole by their art, has the effect of reinforcing to viewers—and enforcing on survivors and descendants—the idea that incarceration, with ingenuity, and aided by the unobtrusive hand of the administration, is endurable. That survivors emerged whole, not in pieces.

"The objects that the Issei and the Nisei made in camp are a physical manifestation of the art of gaman," writes Delphine Hirasuna in *The Art of Gaman*, "testaments to their perseverance, their resourcefulness, their spirit and humanity." But also, as Karen Ishizuka writes, "gaman should not be the primary message of one of the most shameful episodes in American history. Indeed, the valorization of gaman may be an unwitting accomplice to the silencing of Japanese Americans, which underlies—and epigenetically fuels—their trauma."[27]

On the wall, next to a display case holding a camera that belonged to Dave Tatsuno—whose footage from Topaz is one of only two home movies on the National Film Registry of the Library of Congress[28]—was a painting by Norman Rockwell, *Golden Rule*, 1961: DO UNTO OTHERS AS YOU WOULD HAVE THEM DO UNTO YOU printed over an image of two dozen people of various races and religions, clothed, unclothed, with or without head coverings. ("I tried to depict all the peoples of the world gathered

---

27. Karen Ishizuka, "Art Saved Us…From What?" *Are the Arts Essential?* (New York: NYU Press, 2002
28. The other is Abraham Zapruder's footage of JFK's assassination. "Zapruder was lucky," Tatsuno said. "He happened to be at the right place at the right time."

together," Rockwell said. I noticed, in his utopic gathering, a geisha, as if she was the first figure that came to Rockwell's mind when imagining a Japanese person.) *Golden Rule* did not appear only once in the museum; it was also hanging near the back. Its first appearance was suspicious, its second, sinister, the *Golden Rules* rivets holding the museum together.

I grew up surrounded by Norman Rockwell. My father, sansei, covered the walls of our house with Rockwell posters. I never understood why, nor did I—nor have I—asked, and maybe it was beyond my father's understanding too. *Girl in Mirror, The County Agent, Outward Bound, Sheriff and Prisoner* occupied the main walls of our house: the front hallway, above the couch, at the top of the stairs. I could not go anywhere without being made to confront them, without being made to feel like I was walking into or emerging from their quaint, claustrophobic deceptions. I grew to interpret them as representing my father's devotion to a kind of Americanism that might have been handed down to him and his siblings by my grandparents, on whom it had been simultaneously forced and withheld, and into which my father might have developed, however unconsciously, a portal through which to disappear. Absent from the Rockwells in our house were all the peoples of the world. Absent was anyone who was not blindingly—blisteringly—white.

It can feel, standing in the back of a historical museum set into the silence of a small town in America, like standing at the end of time, like you are in danger of falling off. The director and I were standing near the second *Golden Rule*, she was showing me pages from the *Millard County Chronicle* circa 1940s, which her father edited, when she told me a story:

She was ten, with her mother in downtown Delta—which is where she was from and had never left—when she overheard a group of women talking about the Japanese man who was murdered in Topaz. Twelve years had passed since Topaz closed, fourteen since Wakasa was murdered, yet the women were talking as if it had happened that morning. Now, nearly a lifetime later, the echo of their conversation filled the museum: "I heard he was walking his dog," I imagined one of the women saying. "I heard he was collecting stones," I imagined another one saying. "I heard he was picking flowers." "I heard he was trying to escape." "I heard he was deaf."

The director knew about Topaz. Her father printed news from Topaz on the front page of the *Chronicle*, marriages and births, sanitized items like that. Her parents were friends with some of the Japanese Americans, invited them over for meals, some of which the Japanese Americans cooked. The director did not know, until that moment downtown, about the murder, and she seemed to be saying, to me, that it was the murder, being passed around a circle of women, that awakened her consciousness to the meaning of Topaz.

"I didn't know my father," she said. "He died when I was very young."

I wanted to ask her about that—about her father, not knowing him; about his work at the paper and his relationship to the Japanese Americans, about what that meant to her. No doubt the story she told me included, inside of it, other stories she could or would not tell, including about her father, his death, how she missed him.

I thought about my grandfather. He was the original reason behind my being at the museum. He died just as I was becoming more aware of his life, and I missed him. Missing him led me to reading and writing about his life, which led to reading and writing about Japanese American history, which led to reading and writing about Japanese

23

American incarceration. In other words, missing him led to this book. And yet this book is not *about* him. I wondered if the director missed her father *in the form of the museum.*

The museum was empty, but I was surrounded by the specter of 10,000 people moving through the galleries in a manner I had witnessed elsewhere, in other exhibitions: examining, with wistful, beatific expressions, each artifact; remembering, out loud, sometimes in whispers, the Japanese Americans they knew—old friends, neighbors, classmates, some dead, some Japanese from Japan, who had never lived in the United States and who had nothing to do with the history—who resolved, in their minds, into emblems of a shameful chapter which had, to them, closed; shaking their heads but ultimately marveling—often with childlike fascination—at how such a thing could have happened, when, amidst calls for it to never happen again, it is happening all the time everywhere.

"The machinery of whiteness constantly deploys violence," writes Christina Sharpe in *Ordinary Notes*, "and in a mirror-register, constantly manufactures wonder, surprise, and innocence in relation to that violence."

Only a painful memory? Maybe *painful memory* is, in the end, the only legitimate museum.

"To unearth haunted treasure, a person needed to have the stamina to sit with pain as if in a garden," writes Ingrid Rojas Contreras in *The Man Who Could Move Clouds*.

In a corner of the courtyard at the back of the museum, on a strip of gravel between the Boy Scouts Hall—relocated from Topaz—with a wooden fence separating it from the alleyway, was a corrugated shed, open on the bottom like one of those fake rocks people have in their yards. To preface our encounter with the stone, or to offer a disclaimer, the director said, "I have apologized many times." She said it twice, but did not say for what or to whom, and seemed to be speaking to someone who was not there. A shadow was drawn, like a shade, down her face. I saw, in the shadow, the toll of her work, and the sincere yet precarious relationship she had with the concentration camp from which her life had become—by will, by chance, by fate, by default—inextricable. She stared at the shed with the look of someone watching a coffin being lowered into a grave, or, more anxiously, coming up.

We lifted the shed. The stone, beneath the shed, was on the wooden pallet. The carpet was still there, as was the yellow rigging strap. The top of the stone was brownish, dark gray. The bottom of the stone was light, almost white. It looked like Matsumoto Hoji's frog (late 1700s).

According to the *Sakuteiki*—the world's oldest book on the subject of gardening, composed during the Heian Period (when Murasaki Shikibu wrote *The Tale of Genji* and Sei Shonagon wrote *The Pillow Book*)—stones have personalities. They have opinions. They think, they feel, and they have ways of communicating their thoughts and feelings. Maybe that is what the Japanese had been doing for hundreds of years, in the meticulous divining and selection and composition of stones into gardens: listening to the stones. Maybe that is, in fact, what gardens are: listening.

I wondered what the stone was thinking and feeling. It seemed embarrassed, I thought, and very solemn in its embarrassment. But then I thought, no, not embarrassed, the stone's injury and its shame cut much deeper than being embarrassed. The stone, resting, or attempting to rest, was being made to witness and endure something beyond its control. It was *humiliated*. The stone, when it was assumed to have been destroyed, inspired contemplation, awe. Since its removal, it had inspired distress, re-division. It had reinspired the rift. The nature of people surrounding it had changed. It seemed that another stone was warranted, a second stone to console the spirit of the first. It occurred to me, thinking about what the *Sakuteiki* has taught us, that the stone was not consulted, that no one had bothered to ask its opinion.

"When I was five, my mother told me the story of Mr. Wakasa," said Patrick Hayashi, an artist born in Topaz. "I didn't understand why she was telling me the story. And I wasn't able to ask her, because she died very young. And then, after she died, my father didn't talk about Topaz at all, because he thought that Topaz had killed my mother. My mother had a rheumatic heart and Topaz just wore her out. And so, I put Mr. Wakasa's story out of my mind. But I'm afraid it got lodged in my body. Because in 1994, I went to an exhibit of internment camp art called *The View From Within*. The first scene that I saw was a landscape of the Sacramento delta, and when I saw it I started to choke up. The next scene was a still life, a vase of flowers, and I choked up even more. And then I turned a corner, and there was a small brush painting done by the brilliant artist Chiura Obata of Mr. Wakasa falling over after he had been shot through the heart"—his hands open, fingers spread, as if pleading with his shadow. "When I looked at it, I started to sob. I couldn't control myself. And I was terribly embarrassed. But everyone around me was sobbing too."[29]

The View From Within, curated by Karin Higa, opened February 19, 1992, the 50th anniversary of Executive Order 9066, and was the first national exhibition of art made in camp. It opened in Los Angeles and traveled to Salt Lake City, Honolulu, Queens. Hayashi saw it in San Jose, California. When I visited him at his house on a hill above Oakland, he gave me a tour of the art on his walls. Many of the pieces were by Obata: landscapes, a rabbit, a waterfall above his toilet. When he showed me the paintings by Obata on the walls of his bedroom, I thought, *he goes to bed every night with Obata, his dreams are watched over by Obata!*

He showed me his own artwork too. A painting of the river the dead must cross to achieve their afterlife, a tower of stones mounded like chipped ice and a white sun shaped like a turtle shell reflected in the river's still water. A series of small, colorful apparitions on black, made with encaustic, a blowtorch and a hair dryer. "Nancy Ukai asked if I would make a drawing of Wakasa's soul," he said, laughing, but he took it seriously. It was an invitation to return to the site not only of Wakasa's death, but of his own birth. He showed me a painting of his mother holding two young boys, his brothers, in Topaz. She is smiling, his brothers are frowning, but his mother's eyes are not smiling, they are frozen, staring far away from her boys, as if into a river, the river not moving.

---

29. Hayashi shared this story at "From Desecration to Consecration: Community-Led Healing," a livestreamed panel discussion hosted by Kimiko Marr and Japanese American Memorial Pilgrimages, February 17, 2022, featuring Hayashi, Claudia Katayanagi, and Masako Takahashi, with a screening of *Murder in the High Desert: The Killing of James Wakasa*, a film by Emiko Omori. Available on YouTube. Hayashi also tells a version of this story in *Last Witnesses: Reflections on the Wartime Internment of Japanese Americans*, edited by Erica Harth. (New York: St. Martin's Press, 2001)

My favorite painting by Chiura Obata is "Setting Sun on Sacramento Valley" (1930), the sun setting riotously over a steel-blue field. The sky is on fire, its flames, branches and tendrils, look like flesh. The grandeur of the sunset might have been meant to be sublime, but is hellish, of nightmares. Obata painted a softer sunset on March 10, 1943, in Topaz. He and his wife Haruko were on their way to the mess hall when, mesmerized by the sunset, he stopped to paint it. The colors are the same as "Setting Sun," but without the flesh. It still looks like fire though, a wave about to break over emptiness.

In the days after Wakasa's murder, people in camp saw, in the sky above where Wakasa was murdered, hinotama: balls of light. Kiyoshi Katsumoto, seven at the time, lived in the same block as Wakasa, Block 36, on the corner of newly minted Cinnabar Avenue and Greasewood Way (denoting, mockingly, paths of dust between barracks). He and his friends were playing after dinner—"in the twilight," he told me—when they saw an orange-white ball "bouncing" around the sky.

"What did it look like?" I asked him.

"It had jagged edges," he said.

"Like flames?"

"No, not like flames."

"Was it translucent?"

"No, it wasn't translucent."

"Was it solid?"

"No, it wasn't solid."

"Was it windy?"

"No, it wasn't windy," Kiyoshi said. It was perfectly clear and, to those who were not there, impossible to see clearly. The hinotama bounced for several minutes then disappeared.

The following night, same thing: an orange-white ball with jagged edges bouncing for several minutes then disappearing. More people saw it the third night. Several minutes, then silence. Even more people the fourth night.

A year earlier (May 9, 1942), while Kiyoshi was waiting with his family to be taken from Centerville to the Tanforan detention center in South San Francisco, a white woman came up to him and took his picture. The elders—in suits and hats and long black coats—are looking down or into the distance, but the boy in the foreground, is staring directly at the camera. "I was more bewildered than anything," Kiyoshi said seventy-three years later in an interview with photographer Paul Kitagaki Jr.[30] Kiyoshi looks, in the picture, with raised eyebrows and a slight frown, distrusting—of the woman, Dorothea Lange, of the reasons she is there—and protective of the elders.

"Tamashii," the elders said. Hinotama were attributed to premonitions of death, the presence of ghosts after death, the release of energy after someone died, and were often seen near crematories and graveyards. "Was it luminous gases arising from the dead body?" Emiko Katsumoto, Kiyoshi's wife, asked, in an essay she wrote for *Topaz Stories*.[31] A gas is produced when there is no remaining space in which to contain something as voluminous and heavy as grief, but Kiyoshi and his friends, happy, at least momentarily, were not aware—not yet—of grieving, certainly not of contributing their share of grief to the larger, camp-wide orchestration.

Hinotama, as anthropologist Marvin Opler notes, "grew in time of community distress."[32] They were also reported in the Poston and Tule Lake camps, and in the camps

30. Paul Kitagaki Jr., *Behind Barbed Wire: Searching for Japanese Americans Incarcerated During World War II* (Chicago: CityFiles Press, 2019)
31. Emiko Katsumoto, "Mystery at Topaz," *Topaz Stories*: topazstories. com/mystery-at-topaz
32. Marvin K. Opler, "Japanese Folk Beliefs and Practices, Tule Lake, California," *Journal of American Folklore*, Vol. 63, No. 250, October-December 1950

in Canada too: "The kids in school said that when old Honma-san died in Bayfarm, there was a ball of fire that came out of the house and then moved off up the mountain," writes Joy Kogawa in *Obasan*.

The translation of an individual life into a collective death was, on the edge of Topaz, immediate. The edge was operative; the Japanese Americans saw, in the hinotama, the violence inherent in what was being delivered to them as *safety*, and they were bound to one another in that illusion.

As Kiyoshi was talking, I could see clearly in his face the face of a boy three-quarters of a century younger. It was not only the face of a boy looking up at an orange-white ball, but a face the orange-white ball was looking at as it bounced around the sky. And I thought, in that moment, that maybe the hinotama was the 2,000-pound stone *in the past*; that the Japanese Americans were looking at something, like a star, that had already burned out. And with that, they were time traveling too.

Hinotama: the concentrated dawn of the dead's afterlife, a period, an appearance, which often requires the strength, however silent and unassuming, of the living to be illuminated.

Hinotama: the celestial manifestation of the grief of the Japanese Americans.

"Some people have suggested that we should all try to come together as a community and move on," Hayashi said, about the stone's removal. "I'm not ready to move on. There's still a lot of pain that's surfacing and that I didn't even know was there. I just want to be alone with the pain for a while. It's already given me a much deeper love for my mother. I now realize she told me the story [about

Wakasa's murder] because she wanted to prepare me for life in a racist society."[33]

🈁

"As I got close to the site, not sure whether to trust the navigation that was telling me to take this dirt road literally to the middle of nowhere, I began to wonder: what was it like for my dad, not even three, to have been brought out here, on some bus or the back of some truck, in the winter of 1942, cold as hell, not sure whether he was going to live or die," said Ronald Kiino.

"I don't think I'll ever be able to forget how silent it was," said Caroline Kimura. "The silence made me realize that back then, you would have heard everything," said Natalie Kimura (Caroline's sister). "I heard the wind rustling through scrub brush," said Tosh Tanaka. "A random white moth was fluttering about," Natalie Kimura continued.

"I saw empty expanses of desert, ant colonies, rusting plumbing pipes protruding through dusty concrete foundations, rusty barbed wire, broken glass," Tosh Tanaka continued. "I saw marbles, beautiful rocks and ceramics buried in the sand," said Diana Emiko Tsuchida. "Little traces of mud and rocks and barbed wire hanging on by a thread," Natalie Kimura continued. "I didn't know until then about the giant biting anthills that littered the landscape," said Kiku Hughes.

"I needed to walk on the same ground my family had walked on, breathe the air and take in the smell of the sagebrush, and see what they saw in the distance every day," said Naomi Kubota Lee. "Because the site still has quite a bit of debris and marks on the ground, we could stand

33. Patrick Hayashi, at the commemoration of the 80th anniversary of Wakasa's murder, Peace Plaza/Japan Town, San Francisco, April 2023

in the barrack where our family was," said Laura Mariko Cheifetz. "At what would have been the threshold before the door was the remnant of a piece of concrete, which bore the initials of my mother, aunts, and their friends," said Meri Mitsuyoshi. "Along the front were the remains of their garden: a border of volcanic rock and a tree snag." "I was able to see where my dad's barrack and various buildings were located: hospital, baseball field, mess hall, etc.," said Lynn Takahashi Franklin. "It sent chills through my body to actually see this site and visualize what life must have been like." "I imagined my grandparents returning from walks with one or two stones, gradually building the perimeter, planting the tree," Meri Mitsuyoshi continued. "I noticed some stones that were placed in a row, a line delineating perhaps a pathway or something decorative around a barrack," Naomi Kubota Lee continued. "I noticed they were rounded stones. And I remember thinking: *Of course they are round. These were carefully selected stones.*"

"When the white sand covered my shoes, I understood why my grandmother disliked it," said Lisa Hernandez. "We walked over the parched earth, sidestepping greasewood," said Ruth Sasaki, "and the land felt cursed, haunted by the spirits of those who had been detained and died there." "Without the original structures, it's not even a ghost town," said Amy Lee-Tai. "It's more like a ghost land. My heart sank to take it in."

"I could feel anger and frustration building up inside of me," Lynn Takahashi Franklin continued. "I felt an overwhelming feeling of despair and sadness," Lisa Hernandez continued. "I felt uneasy and uncomfortable, which really surprised me," Diana Emiko Tsuchida continued, "like I was alone in an environment that was just so fraught with sadness, bitterness and heartache." "To my surprise, my legs collapsed underneath me," said Nancy Ukai, "and I began to sob." "I just burst into tears," said Kimiko Marr.

"I kept thinking about how time merely exists as a witness to unspeakable things," said Natalie Kimura.

Natalie Kimura and Caroline Kimura had at least ten family members in Topaz, including their grandfather. Kimiko Marr had more than twenty family members in Topaz. Nancy Ukai had sixteen family members in Topaz, including her mother. Diana Emiko Tsuchida had three family members in Topaz, including her father. Lisa Hernandez had five family members in Topaz, including her mother. Lynn Takahashi Franklin had three family members in Topaz, including her father. Amy Lee-Tai had five family members in Topaz, including her mother. Ruth Sasaki had ten family members in Topaz, including her mother. Naomi Kubota Lee had nine family members in Topaz, including her parents. Meri Mitsuyoshi had ten family members in Topaz, including her parents. Laura Mariko Cheifetz had several family members in Topaz, including her grandmother and great-grandfather. Kiku Hughes had three family members in Topaz, including her grandmother. Tosh Tanaka had seven family members in Topaz, including his mother. Ronald Kiino had three family members in Topaz, including his father, who was three when he was playing with a friend beneath guard tower eight, heard shouting above, and looked up.

"All that past broken and discarded stuff, every rock and stone, belongs to the place, to be left untouched, scorched by sun, weathered, and returned to the earth, an archeological site whose desolate surface memory is now a sacred memorial," writes Karen Tei Yamashita, in "KonMarimasu," about her visit to Topaz.[34]

34. Karen Tei Yamashita, "KonMarimasu," *Sansei and Sensibility* (Minneapolis, MN: Coffee House Press, 2020)

"A memory is too powerful a weapon," Kiku Hughes writes in *Displacement*. Next to these words, orange flowers, growing out of the desert, cast a shadow that extends to the edge of the page, off the page and out of the book. The stone did not disappear. It was not lost or hiding from history or the future. It was, when it was found, where it was last touched.

"This is a sign from your ancestors," Mary Farrell said, to Nancy Ukai.

"This is their voice," Ukai said, of the Issei.[35]

When I told the filmmaker Emiko Omori, who was a child in Poston, what I read in the *Sakuteiki* about the stone having opinions, and that maybe one way to resolve the question of what should be done with the stone would be to ask it, she said: "The stone has done its job."

Later, in an email, she revised what she said: "I should have said that the stone is doing its job."

Some people have said that the stone is one of the most important artifacts of Japanese American incarceration. Some people have said it's just a rock. ("Except for its extraordinary symbolism, it looks remarkably ordinary," wrote one descendant of Topaz;[36] on the contrary, "even the most ordinary rock / carries a history / rapturous as the stars," writes Amy Uyematsu in her poem "Sister Stone"). Some people have suggested, more generally, that the community needs to *move on*. Some people feel that when the stone was removed, the community was deprived of the opportunity to heal, and that without healing, there can be no legitimate or enduring way to move on.

Heal: to make whole, return to wholeness. The community, with its identifications and misidentifications, inclusions and exclusions, is not, and will never be, monolithic. It is composed, rather, of an outward-spreading infinity of

35. Ukai and Farrell, *Uncovering a 78-year-old Mystery*, op cit.
36. nichibei.org/2022/02/in-praise-of-j-a-allies/

thoughts and feelings. It could be understood, in this formulation, that the stone was not the projection of survivors and descendants of Topaz, but they were the projection of the stone—shaped and shifting, moving and changing color, according to the memorials formed to console them.

The memorial is not only the stone, but what happens because of it. And it is not only that we, with our energy and vigilance, are protecting the stone, but that the stone is protecting us.

"Some powerful force emanates from the stone," Emiko said, "and we are awash in its force..."

"As for the hearts / they've remained neutral like fence flowers," writes the Palestinian poet Mahmoud Darwish, in his poem "A State of Siege."[37] The day I visited the site where Wakasa was murdered, where the stone had been peeking out of the ground, thin weeds with tiny yellow flowers were growing out of the depression. They were unassuming yet determined. I heard rustling. I gripped two strands of barbed wire, squeezed them together, and stepped over the fence—I broke *back into* camp—and walked up to the depression. Depression, but it was a hole, robbed of what it had carried, and melancholic with that loss. I imagined sinking, but instead of becoming lodged in the earth, falling, like Alice down the rabbit hole.

I did not want to leave but I did not want to stay. I wanted to stay forever but I resented having had to travel so far to get there. The story is much longer and much shorter than this. How to tell it without forsaking what happened after the story ended? The site that tells the story not of innocence and perseverance, but of white supremacy, murder, and the never-ending contest and crisis of

37. Mahmoud Darwish, "A State of Siege," *The Butterfly's Burden*, translated from the Arabic by Fady Joudah. (Port Townsend, WA: Copper Canyon Press, 2007)

memorialization, is a hole—slightly discolored, increasingly subliminal—in the desert. It was windy. I could see rainstorms in several directions. I touched the depression. It was soft, like cake flour, and warm.

no museum

no monument

no poem
no song
can house
the spirit
of a passed soul...

TRACI KATO-KIRIYAMA
"No Redress"

...only love can help you recognize what you do not
remember

JAMES BALDWIN
The Evidence of Things Not Seen

PEACE PLAZA

A WOMAN WITH A RED SCARF CAME UP TO ME IN THE
Peace Plaza in Japantown, San Francisco. I was standing
at the entrance to the mall, reading a timeline mounted
on the wall: "1948–1960: About ½ of Japantown is razed
for one of the first major federally funded 'urban renewal'
projects in the United States. Nearly 1,500 Japanese Americans and over 60 businesses are displaced." Three years
after the war, two years after the last of the concentration camps (Tule Lake) closed, and shortly after returning
to the cities and towns from which they had been forcibly
removed, the Japanese Americans were, once again, being
displaced. Before the war, there were 43 Japantowns in California alone. Three remain: in Los Angeles, San Jose, San
Francisco.

It was a cold afternoon in August. I heard a voice.
"Thank you for reading the timeline." I turned around to
see a woman in a red scarf. The way she said "Thank you"
made me think that she had written the timeline, had at
least been involved in its making.

The most conspicuous feature of the Peace Plaza is the
five-story pagoda. It was designed by Yoshiro Taniguchi,
and was a gift, twenty years after the war, from Japan. Of

Taniguchi's famous works, most of which are in Tokyo, many of which are in Kanazawa, the pagoda is the only one outside of Japan. It was modeled, in form, after the Hyakumanto Darani, miniature pagodas, each containing a Buddhist text, that were commissioned by Empress Koken in the eighth century. (She commissioned one million.) On windy days, the pagoda becomes a wind instrument. The Asian American High School Students Alliance had, that afternoon, set up three taiko drums adorned with purple dragons beneath the pagoda, but the students were nowhere to be found. A short distance away, much less conspicuous, is a slender three-sided bronze sculpture. It stands on the sidewalk on Post Street, like a pedestrian waiting to cross. It was made by Louis Quaintance and Eugene Daub, white men, and consists of three bas-relief panels, each depicting a scene of Japanese American life: a family—man with cabbage, woman with broom, girl with doll; women dancing at a festival; people being driven out of their communities. Quaintance's website refers to the scenes as "dramas" that illustrate "the very real sacrifices, sturggles [misspelled], and eventual survival, and celebration, of Japanese Americans."[38] The same sculpture stands in Japantown in Los Angeles and San Jose. It was funded by the Civil Liberties Public Education Program, created by the Civil Liberties Act of 1988. "The artist's task," Quaintance's website continues, "was to succinctly, expressively, and honestly communicate this story," but why was the task entrusted to two white men, and what, exactly, is the story?

The woman with the red scarf was sansei, maybe twenty years older than me. Her name was Marianne, which she

---

38. Last I checked, the majority of Quaintance's website was devoted to a memorial he and Daub made for the USS *San Diego*, a ship instrumental in the war with Japan.

pronounced "Mary-AHN." Her grandfather immigrated to the United States through Seattle. He eventually immigrated to Beijing, where he died. Her accent kept changing: Japanese, Chinese, British, Southern. When I told her my name, she said it back to me, exaggeratedly, "BRAHN-DAHN." And when I told her that I was writing a book about Japanese American incarceration, she shook her head and said: "We're beyond that."

What does it mean for people to survive a trauma, and how can anyone be sure that they have survived, rather than, more simply, not died? If people have transformed beyond who and how they were before the threat became real and started moving through them, what can be said to have survived, on the far side of that transformation? And what does it mean to celebrate on that far side, when everyone—in the sky, beneath the ground, or at the bottom of the sea—whose death or disappearance might attest to something different, something not deserving of celebration, is no longer present, or has been forced, by the people who have hurried themselves into the celebratory "beyond," to remain in the past?

At the bottom of the panel of women dancing is a poem by Janice Mirikitani, one of the first Japanese American poets I read, one of the first, for me, who existed. She was an infant when her family was incarcerated in Rohwer, in the flood plain of the Mississippi. The poem is called "Footsteps lead to destiny":

> We dance honoring ancestors
> who claim our home,
> and freedom to pursue our dreams.
> Our voices carve a path for justice:
> Equal rights for all.

We prevail.
Our future harvested from generations.

From my life
opens countless lives.

The Journey continues...

Who was Marianne speaking for when she said, "We're
beyond that?" Her presence in the Peace Plaza, and her
thanking me for me being there, did not suggest that she
was *beyond* at least having an interest in the history of
Japantown and playing a role in sharing it. I wished I had
the courage or wit or presence of mind, or sympathy, to ask
Marianne if she thought it was possible to move *beyond* an
event that has not ended without abandoning all the individuals still mired within it, and without making peace,
however uncomfortable, with that abandonment, but I did
not say anything. I smiled and felt ashamed—of myself, of
the book that I wanted, right then, to put down, and for
wanting to put the book down. What I meant to say—but
it was too late, the red scarf was flying around the corner—
was a book *about the ongoing afterlife of*...

On Saturday, June 22, 2019, Japanese Americans gathered in
front of Bentley Gate on the edge of Fort Sill, an army base
outside Lawton, Oklahoma, to protest the Trump administration's plan to reopen the base as a detention facility
to incarcerate approximately 1,600 asylum-seeking children from Central America. The protest was organized by
Tsuru for Solidarity, a Japanese American–led social justice organization committed to interrupting state violence,
ending migrant detention, closing all detention sites, supporting immigrant and refugee communities. Among the

protesters were survivors in their 70s and 80s. Satsuki Ina, co-founder and co-chair of Tsuru for Solidarity, spoke first.

"I am a former child incarceree," she began. "We are here today to protest the repetition of history. We were held under indefinite detention. We were without due process of law. We were charged without any evidence of being a threat to national security, that we were an unassimilable race, that we would be a threat to the economy. We hear these exact words today regarding innocent people seeking asylum in this country."

Satsuki's parents, Shizuko and Itaru, were incarcerated in Tanforan, Topaz, and Tule Lake, where Itaru was held in the maximum-security stockade, and where he wrote haiku, including:

itotonbo	Damselflies—
haya umareshi-ka	already born
goku no mado	at the prison window[39]

Satsuki was born in Tule Lake, into the impossible status of being simultaneously a citizen and an enemy of the United States. Her testimony was followed by that of other survivors, each wearing a #StopRepeatingHistory T-shirt and holding an enlarged photo of themselves as a child.

"I spent my first four-and-a-half years in a concentration camp," said Kiyoshi Ina, Satsuki's older brother. "I'm here to protest the incarceration of immigrant children."

"On December 7, 1941, I was celebrating my fourth birthday," said Nikki Nojima Louis, "when the FBI interrupted my party and removed my father to Lordsburg, New Mexico. My mother and I were incarcerated at the Puyallup Fairgrounds, called *Camp Harmony*, and later in Minidoka."

---

39. Written July 2, 1945; translated by Hisako Ifshin and Leza Lowitz, and published in *Modern Haiku*, Volume 34.2, Summer 2003

As if on cue, she was interrupted again, this time by a military police officer demanding that the protest move across the highway.

"Let's go," he shouted. "Today!"

"Otherwise what will happen?" Satsuki asked.

"I don't know," he said, surprisingly. Why didn't he know? The question could not have been simpler. "I'm not going to arrest you," he said, "but you need to move now."

"If you're not going to arrest us, we're not going to move," said Mike Ishii, co-founder and co-chair of Tsuru for Solidarity. When I asked him about this moment, he told me that behind a stone wall that read WELCOME TO FORT SILL, OKLAHOMA, there were approximately thirty additional police officers, armed and waiting.

The survivors were arranged in a line. Beside them stood Duncan Ryuken Williams, Zen Buddhist priest. Behind them, a line of descendants—Aura Newlin, Karen Ishizuka, Nancy Ukai, Lauren Sumida, Martha Nakagawa, Ruth Sasaki, among them—holding up a rope from which were hanging many garlands of colorful tsuru. In front of them were cameras, reporters, local activist groups, including Black Lives Matter Oklahoma City, led by T. Sheri Dickerson.

Before the protest, Ishii led a civil disobedience training. He explained to the survivors that there was a chance that they would be arrested, and if that were to happen, there was no guarantee how much, or how little, they would be protected. The survivors were asked if they wanted to go through with the protest. One by one, each survivor said *Yes*.

"I spent three-and-a-half years at Poston, an American concentration camp," said Chizu Omori. "I'm here to bear witness to the travesty of the American justice system."

"This is me in 1943," said Paul Tomita, holding an enlargement of his Indefinite Leave card, issued on July 4, 1943, permitting him to leave Minidoka. He was four.

The MP, a large man, yet diminishing in stature, interrupted again. "It's English!" he shouted. "Get out!"

Paul, wearing a T-shirt with the words "No-No" emblazoned in black between strands of barbed wire, kept talking.

"Can you please describe what's happening?" a reporter asked Satsuki.

"They're wanting to remove us," she said. "We've been removed too many times."

For whatever they were feeling individually, together the survivors projected indomitable confidence and calm. The MP was flustered, losing faith. What, in the face of a group of steadfast elders, speaking solemnly and assuredly from the perspective of people who had already been arrested, who had already been removed too many times, was the MP supposed to do? He had become, despite his station and his weapons, defenseless. "His violence came up against our moral authority of nonviolence," Ishii told me.

The MP, summoning the last of his weakening will, shouted, "What don't you people understand?!"

"We understand the whole history of this country," Reiko Redmonde shouted back, "and we aren't going to let it happen again!"

The Japanese Americans were speaking not only on behalf of themselves, but on behalf of the 707 Issei who were incarcerated at Fort Sill, 1941–1942, including many Buddhist and Shinto priests. I first heard of Fort Sill because of my interest in a man named Ichiro Shimoda. A gardener from Los Angeles, Shimoda died, under mysterious circumstances, in Fort Sill. His story, which exists in the historical record in contradictory fragments, is that he witnessed the murder of another Issei, Kanesaburo Oshima, a shopkeeper from Hawaii, who also died in Fort Still—shot and killed by a guard. According to one account, Shimoda suffered a

45

nervous breakdown as a result, and was taken to the military hospital, where he died. None of the other prisoners were with him, and nothing else about the incident is known. Shimoda's death, with Oshima's murder, was folded efficiently into the oblivion on which the carceral system thrives. No guards stood trial or were held accountable.

That was not how it began. Approximately 340 Chiricahua Apaches were incarcerated at Fort Sill between 1894 and 1914. Among them was the Apache leader Geronimo, who is buried there, in the Bear Creek Apache cemetery. ("Which means," Kathy Kojimoto told me, "you must go to the military base visitors center, fill out paperwork, have valid photo ID, and get a pass" to visit Geronimo's grave. "This includes the descendants of the tribe.") Fort Sill was also the site of a Native American boarding school (opened in 1871, closed in 1980) which separated Indigenous children from their families, forcing them into a program of cultural erasure and reidentification.

"It didn't work," said Lavetta Yeahquo, an elder of the Kiowa Tribe of Oklahoma, who had gone through the boarding school system. "We still have our language, we still have dances, we still have our songs, we're still here."

During the Obama administration, approximately 1,200 migrant children from Central America were incarcerated at Fort Sill; the Department of Health and Human Services (HHS) eventually closed the detention center, citing the "exceptional expense" of keeping it running. Most of the children the government incarcerated then, and was seeking to incarcerate in 2019, crossed the US–Mexico border with family, half of them with parents already in the United States, yet they were classified as unaccompanied. They were held in overcrowded cages, then moved to less visible, more indefinite camps—outposts of the border wall—where they were deprived of the basic dignities that might have reminded them that there was, beyond the care they were able to offer each other, a world, and that the world cared.

I asked Satsuki how she felt being at Fort Sill. "I found my suffocated voice," she said. Though she was not incarcerated there, it was as though her childhood had been dispersed across the geography of incarceration, and that her voice, preceding her, was waiting. "Anger rose to the top of the sorrow," she said.

A month later, a coalition of immigrant youth, members of Indigenous, Latinx, Black, Jewish, and Asian American communities, returned to Fort Sill. Buddhist priests, led by Williams, chanted sutras for "the Japanese immigrants who passed away during their WWII incarceration; to all those who suffered at Fort Sill in the past; to the ten children who have died in the border crossing or in custody of the US Border Patrol and other agencies in the past fourteen months; to all the migrants who are facing such difficult circumstances currently."[40]

Four days later, Senator Jim Inhofe announced that the plan to use the base to incarcerate migrant children was being put on hold. Two days after that, the Administration for Children and Families, a division of HHS, claimed that, due to a decrease in migrant children crossing the border, there was no longer "an immediate need to place children in influx facilities."

On Saturday, March 6, 2021, another group of Japanese Americans gathered, this time virtually, to speak out about migrant detention. All but one of the participants were teenagers. The oldest of them, the host of the event, was Skyla Sachiko Tomine (17), high school student, activist, and Satsuki Ina's granddaughter.

40. Duncan Ryūken Williams, "July Protest: Buddhist Clergy and Lay Leaders x Tsuru for Solidarity x United We Dream July 20, 2019: A Buddhist Memorial Service as Protest," duncanryukenwilliams.com

The first presenter was Ivan Ramirez (14), a member of the indigenous Mayan Mam from Guatemala, who was calling from a church in Austin, where he and his mother Hilda were living in sanctuary. They fled Guatemala when he was seven, were detained in the Dilley detention center (Texas) for almost a year, and had been living in the church for almost five years. Ivan showed a video that he made that told his and his mother's story. In it, he described living in a child migrant detention center. La Perrera, he called it, the dog kennel. He described the food, the worms in the food, which Ivan illustrated, in the video, with rainbow-colored gummy worms in a bowl of black beans. "Maybe they fell down," the guards said, about the worms. From the ceiling? "Just eat it," the guards demanded. Children were constantly getting sick, fainting, vomiting. "If you got sick, they would not care," Ivan said. When the children were not able to eat, the guards claimed that they refused. Sometimes the children refused; they went on hunger strike. The guards were constantly screaming at them, holding guns to them if they misbehaved or spoke out. Sometimes the children spoke out; they protested, shouted "Libéranos!"

"When I came here I was nine," Ivan said, of the church. "And now I'm fourteen. I don't know when I'm going to have a normal life and when I'm going to get free."

Skyla asked Ivan what people could do to help him and his mother. "Tell Biden to stop our deportation, stop the detention centers, stop deporting people," he said.

Ivan was followed by Mina Loy Akira Checel (13), an aspiring filmmaker and the granddaughter of Karen Ishizuka, activist, writer, and chief curator at the Japanese American National Museum (JANM), and Robert Nakamura, filmmaker. Checel showed a video she made for a school project on family separation, including its connection to Japanese American incarceration. "There are about 69,550 children who have been separated miles away from their parents, whom the US government is failing to reunite," she said.

"They are living in harsh conditions, no ways to take baths, and barely enough food. They are in prison."

As Checel's film was playing, I could see Ivan, in his Zoom rectangle on the edge of my screen, looking apprehensively out the window. Then he turned his camera off. At the end of the event, when he and his mother turned their camera back on, Hilda was visibly shaken. Holding back tears, she explained in Spanish what had happened. The writer Aida Salazar translated: "Ivan and Hilda had to turn off the camera because there was a man who was threatening them, who was trying to burn down the church. He's angry at their existence. That just happened, right now."

As I think about the people, like Ivan and Hilda, who are attempting to fashion a future in the face of desperate odds and the anger of strangers who want to burn their sanctuaries to ash; as I think about people, like Tomine and Checel, descendants of incarceration, who exist, in a certain way, in the realization of a version of that future, and are creating, of that realization, other forms of sanctuary—stories, for example, and the opportunity to tell them; as I think about the children and grandchildren and great-grandchildren who have been developing and sharpening their awareness of the connections between crimes against being human, and who have been upholding, through demonstrations and acts of solidarity, the energy that has been passed down to them; as I think about the Japanese American elders protesting at sites of exception—Fort Sill; ICE headquarters in San Francisco; the ICE detention center at the Yuba County Jail in Marysville; Cook County Jail in Chicago; the Greensboro Piedmont Academy in North Carolina; the Berks County detention center in Pennsylvania; the Carrizo Springs, Dilley, and Fort Bliss migrant detention centers in Texas; the Northwest detention center in Tacoma, Washington; and so on and ongoing; as I think about the people who have been thinking about and standing in solidarity with and taking direct action to support the people who are living and dying, today and tonight, under the watch and the weight of their oppressors; and as I think about the people who are not thinking about those people, because they do not have the knowledge or time, or because they do not want to, or because they refuse to, or because they do not believe in the struggle, or because they condone or endorse, in one form or another, the oppression, or because they have not yet reached the imperative opening at the end of their own storytelling, I am led to believe that Japanese American incarceration, as one example in an unremitting, insatiable anthropocene of exception, has not ended, but has entered a new phase...

The filmmaker Rea Tajiri was once asked, "Aren't you tired of being an internment artist?" Tajiri has made two of my favorite films: *History and Memory: For Akiko and Takashige* (1991), a short, speculative documentary; and *Strawberry Fields* (1997), a feature-length fiction film, both of which find their source in Tajiri's family's—especially her mother's—incarceration in Santa Anita and Poston. It was the kind of question that might shame a person into reexamining their obsessions and the reasons why they are unable to exorcise them, but it was not a question.

"Will you write the same poem forever?" writes Michael Prior, in the voice of another poet, in his poem, "Broken Record."

"Why bring it back? / The camps are over" writes David Mura, in the voice of his mother, in his poem "An Argument: On 1942." "David, it was so long ago—how useless it seems."

"I'm worn. I'm tired / of their histories," writes Brynn Saito, in the voice of a stone, in her poem "Stone Returns, 70 Years Later."

"I'm tired of walking around," says Kiku Hughes in *Displacement*. She is visiting Japantown San Francisco with her mother. They are trying to find the house where Kiku's grandmother grew up. They have the address, but keep getting lost, because the house is gone, replaced by the Peace Plaza. Kiku's mother consoles herself by checking out the mall. Kiku, tired, sits on a rock in the shadow of the pagoda and closes her eyes.

"That's when it happened. I heard the music first. And then when I opened my eyes, all I could see was a thick fog. But when it cleared at last...I was somewhere entirely different."

In a dark theater. Kiku, bewildered, is sitting in the audience, surrounded by people in clothing of a different era. On the stage, a young girl is playing violin. She is introduced as Ernestina Teranishi. "Teranishi," Kiku says to herself. "I knew that name." The moment Kiku realizes that she has been transported into the presence of her grandmother as a young girl, the fog returns and sends her back to the present.

In Kimiko Guthrie's novel *Block Seventeen*, Jane, a sansei descendant of Rohwer, falls asleep in the middle of the afternoon. She wakes up to find herself in a disorienting, moss-covered place, "pitch black," with a "sulfuric stench," populated by blue shadows, humanoid figures, towers made of small objects, newspapers, a wooden boat, and her mother, but her mother when her mother was young. That Jane finds herself in this uncanny place, confronted with loaded fragments of an opaque history, is a consequence of her knowing next to nothing about her family's experience, and that lack of knowing pressing against her. "It seemed I'd fallen into some wet, prehistoric hole near the center of the earth."

BEST WISHES
FOR THE FUTURE

THE REPARATIONS MY GRANDFATHER RECEIVED FROM the United States government were used to pay for his first year in the nursing home where he spent the last five years of his life. My grandmother received a check for $20,000. She spent it on my grandfather's rent. He never saw it. He did not know anything about it. He was ten years into Alzheimer's. He did not know he had, fifty years earlier, been classified as an enemy alien of the United States and incarcerated in a Department of Justice prison under suspicion of being a spy for Japan. The check was a coin placed in my grandfather's mouth. It came with a letter: a form apology from the White House. It was not addressed to my grandfather. It was not addressed to anyone. It was stamped with the signature of George H. W. Bush. The last sentence read: "You and your family have our best wishes for the future."

Five years later my grandfather was dead. His funeral was held in a nondescript church in North Carolina. The church was filled with people my grandfather did not know or would not have remembered. There was a small number of Japanese Americans, but they were outnumbered by white people, some of whom were there to support my grandmother, most of whom were on their way into the sanctuary when they caught a glimpse of the photograph, surrounded by flowers, of an Asian man they recognized but did not know, and thought, with fleeting sympathy, *He's dead.*

I was not there. I was eighteen, first year in college, upstate New York. My mother called. "You don't need to go," she said. I believed her. Or I believed that my grandfather, who had long since lost his mind, was already dead, and that I had made my peace with his being gone, which quickly proved to be untrue.

When I was young, I did not know anything about Japanese American incarceration. I was not, as a young person—or a person, in general—uncommon in this. Not only did I not know anything about Japanese American incarceration, I did not know that my grandfather had been incarcerated, nor that other members of my family were also incarcerated: my great-aunt Joy in Poston; my great-uncle Makio (Roy), great-aunt Tsuruyo (Pearl), and their daughters, Sally and Carole, in Heart Mountain; my great-aunt Setsuko's family in Manzanar.

I do not remember when I first heard of *internment*, which was the only word that seemed to exist. I do not remember if I heard it at home, from my parents, at my grandparents' house, at school. I have a vague memory of a small gray box in my ninth-grade US History textbook, stating, in one lackluster paragraph, a wartime, therefore justifiable, injustice. In the white town in Connecticut where I grew up (compositionally synonymous with the white town where my grandfather died), I might have been the only one who could see it. I do not remember if my classmates looked at me. I remember *internment* had something to do with my grandfather. He might as well have been the whole story.

54

I was one of only two Asian Americans in my elementary school. The other was my sister, two grades older. Among the names my classmates called me was Mr. Miyagi. 1985, 1986. Never mind that Mr. Miyagi was old, bald, had facial hair and a Japanese accent; he was a new and convenient reference with which white boys could try out their racism as comedy. I knew, from the credits of *The Karate Kid*, that Mr. Miyagi was played by Noriyuki "Pat" Morita, but I did not know that Morita was American, and that his accent was part of his character. I did not know that when Morita was young he was in an internment camp. It was not until years later that I learned that it was not an *internment* camp, but a *concentration* camp; that internment refers to the detention of non-citizens, while incarceration refers to the detention of citizens; that two-thirds of the people who were incarcerated were citizens and that the other third were not citizens because they were not eligible, by law, to become citizens; and that therefore the difference between being incarcerated and being interned was, for those who were not citizens—many of whom had lived in the United States for decades—outside of their control.

I did not know that children were incarcerated. When Morita was two, he was diagnosed with spinal TB. He spent the next decade in a body cast in the Weimar Sanatorium, northeast of Sacramento, then in the Shriners Hospital in San Francisco. When his family was incarcerated in Gila River, the FBI picked him up and carried him to camp. He cried the first four days. "I was homesick for the hospital," he said. "I could feel and sense and hear all the colors and horrors of incarceration. The sadness, the hopelessness." Many years later, he returned to Gila River. His wife Evelyn remembers him breaking down. He told her that "a day didn't go by that you didn't hear about a suicide or a stillborn or somebody dying from an illness they couldn't treat."[41]

---

41. *More Than Miyagi: The Pat Morita Story*, dir. Kevin Derek, 2021

One night, at his house, Mr. Miyagi gets drunk and tells Daniel (Ralph Macchio) that he had a wife, that she was in a concentration camp, Manzanar, and that she had just given birth. "First American-born Miyagi," he says, before passing out. He is holding a piece of paper. Daniel removes it from his hand. A telegram. He reads it: "We regret to inform you that on November 2, 1944 at the Manzanar Relocation Center, your wife and newborn son died due to complications arising from childbirth." Miyagi received the telegram in Europe. He was in the 442nd, the segregated, all-Nisei combat unit.[42] That scene in *Karate Kid* seemed to indicate where the Japanese Americans had gone, and where, as represented by Mr. Miyagi, they were forced to keep going. The formula seemed to be that for a citizen to be born, an immigrant had to be struck down; and the citizen dies anyway. Because I was introduced to these things by a movie, and because the movie was not really about any of these things, Japanese American incarceration was introduced to me as fiction. It was my least favorite scene in *The Karate Kid*. Too dark, too slow, motivated by too much history. It brought the world into the room.

Then it was my grandmother and me. June Shimoda, born Chizuko Yamashita. Her parents were from Fukuoka, both named Yamashita (no relation), and both contract laborers—he as a railroad worker, she as his wife, a picture bride.

My grandmother was not incarcerated. She was born and, except for two years in Fukuoka, raised on a farm in Utah, outside the exclusion zone. The fact that she was not incarcerated and my grandfather was, underscored, in my mind, a difference between them. There were Japanese Americans who were free and Japanese Americans who

---

42. November 2, 1944: seven leaders of the Fair Play Committee in Heart Mountain, a group of more than sixty Nisei who organized in resistance to the draft, are sentenced to prison for draft evasion.

were not, but I did not know what constituted the difference—gender? generation? citizenship? suspicion? None of these interpretations included racism—that is, none included white people—as if incarceration was a matter of immaculate misfortune.

I interviewed my grandmother in 1999. I was in undergraduate school, taking a class, my first, on Asian American history. The stories she told me became the genesis of my book, *The Grave on the Wall*. We sat in the living room where I saw my grandfather for the last time and stared out the sliding glass doors into the trees.[43] My grandmother told me about picnics with other families from Fukuoka. I heard the sound of parents gossiping in Japanese. I did not hear, in their gossip, the distance between the Issei and Nisei, nor did I hear gossip as commiseration. I did not see the Issei disappearing through the gossip into Fukuoka, nor the Nisei disappearing into a country that was just as foreign. Instead I felt the pangs of sadness about having missed out on what I perceived as the halcyon days of Japanese America. About having missed out not only on what it meant to be Japanese American, but on being a contributor to its meaning. I felt seedless and pale, the diminishment of being Japanese in favor of being American. That I, a biracial yonsei, represented, in the form of the future looking back, its mourner and nullification, both the destiny and attenuation of Japanese America.

82,219 Japanese Americans received reparations in the form of $20,000, to account, as a formality, for what they had lost. Or, because loss is a euphemism for theft, what had been stolen. The Office of Redress Administration, created

43. Brandon Shimoda, *The Grave on the Wall* (San Francisco: City Lights, 2019)

by the Civil Liberties Act—the culmination of a multi-generational struggle, which included the testimonies of more than 500 survivors, many of whom were confronting, articulating, and sharing their experiences for the first time—paid out 1.6 billion dollars. The first nine checks were presented to nine of the oldest prisoners in a ceremony in DC, October 9, 1990. Checks 10 through 82,219, accompanied by letters without names or salutations, were delivered from 1991 to 1993.

Mamoru Eto, a 107-year-old Issei living in the Keiro Nursing Home in Los Angeles (where my great-grandmother, Asano Yamashita, also lived, and died), was the first to receive a check. Eto immigrated to the United States in 1919 (the same year as my grandfather). He and his wife, Kura, settled in Pasadena, where they had ten children.[44] Eto worked on a farm and preached during the winter, to migrant laborers mostly, farm to farm. He opened the First Japanese Nazarene Church in his living room. He and seven of his children—three had already left California; Kura had returned, alone, to Japan—were incarcerated in Tulare and Gila River. Even though he was not, at the time, eligible for US citizenship, Eto forswore his allegiance to Japan. "We're not Japanese anymore," he said. "We're American," adding: "There's no other way."[45]

---

44. One of his children, his son Ken, was the highest-ranking Asian American in the Chicago Outfit, the mob syndicate founded by Al Capone. He learned how to gamble while incarcerated in Minidoka, and later ran a gambling racket in Chicago. It was broken up by the FBI. An assassination attempt, from inside the Outfit, was made on Ken's life. He survived three shots to the back of his head. He agreed to become an informant for the FBI. The investigation was called Operation Sun-Up. He testified, in black hood with eyeholes, against fifteen of his associates. They all went to prison. Eto entered the Witness Protection Program, and died, in 2004, under the pseudonym Joe Tanaka. His aliases included: Joe Montana, Joe Eto, John Ito, Joe Nakamura, Joe Keneto, Tokyo Joe, Joe the Jap, and The Chinaman.

45. Barbara Koh, "Breaking the Long Silence: Mamoru Eto," *Los Angeles Times*, November 25, 1990.

"Do you know what your family members did with the reparations?" I asked the descendants. "They bought a new roof," they answered. "They built a front porch. They fixed the patio. Repaved the driveway. Installed a new drainage system. A trash compactor. Hardwood floors. Floor-length curtains. They bought folding screens. A leather recliner. A camera lens. Golf club membership. Fishing equipment. Farm equipment. Groceries. They paid bills. Ambulance bills. Hospital bills. Car loans. Mortgages. They paid for a down payment on a house. Private school. College funds. A film degree. A music therapy degree. Weddings. Long-term care insurance. Assisted living. They bought stocks. Savings bonds. They gave it to their children. Their siblings. Grandchildren. They drank it away. Gambled it away. They went to Japan. Four trips to Japan. (Their first time back.) (Their first time visiting.) To Hiroshima. To China. To Singapore. To Egypt. To Norway. To Peru. To Brazil. To Portugal. On a religious pilgrimage to Fátima. To Spain. To France. On a religious pilgrimage to Lourdes. To Canada. To Mexico. To Hawaii. To Alaska. They started a teriyaki sauce business. An auto repair business. They bought a log cabin. A customized van. A red truck. A Honda Civic. A Nissan Maxima. A Mazda 626. An Acura. A Lexus ES 350. A Toyota Camry. A Toyota Corolla. They donated it to the local community center. The local library (for a collection of books about incarceration). The Red Cross. The Christian church. The Buddhist Church. The Buddhist Churches of America. The JACL. JANM. They split it. They did not want it. They never spent it. They gave it away."

"The United States is not *at war*. The United States *is* war," writes Sora Han, professor of criminology and law.

"Necessity has no law," wrote Gratian, a 4th-century Roman emperor. Gratian makes an appearance in Giorgio Agamben's *State of Exception*, in which "state of exception" is elucidated not as a temporary suspension of law but as a permanent paradigm of government. Historian Clinton Rossiter explains this paradigm as "crisis government," ruled by "constitutional dictatorship." He calls Japanese American incarceration an "assertion of dictatorial power." Agamben calls it a "spectacular violation of civil rights," and quotes the eighth of Walter Benjamin's Theses on the Philosophy of History, that "the tradition of the oppressed teaches us that the *state of emergency* in which we live is not the exception but the rule."

The motivation for incarceration was propagandized as "military necessity." The Civil Liberties Act recognized the motivation as "racial prejudice, wartime hysteria, and a failure of political leadership," which was, and still is, an apt definition of the basic climate of the United States. These determinations were made by the Commission on Wartime Relocation and Internment of Civilians (CWRIC), established by Congress in 1982 to investigate Executive Order 9066. EO 9066, signed by Franklin Delano Roosevelt, was five short paragraphs. It authorized the Secretary of War (today's Secretary of Defense) to designate military areas "from which any or all persons may be excluded," and to provide, for those persons, transportation (to where?), food (what kind?), shelter (where? what kind? how long?). It stated, as justification, that "the successful prosecution of the war requires every possible protection against espionage and sabotage." It did not cite a single instance of either. It did not mention removal or incarceration, detention centers or concentration camps, Japanese immigrants or Japanese Americans. As is standard for racist legislation, it targeted a specific population, while keeping itself flexible for future emergencies.

The CWRIC consisted of nine people, eight men, one woman, all but one of whom were white. William Marutani was a teenager when he was incarcerated in the Pinedale detention center, then Tule Lake. "If they stepped out of line," Marutani said, of the other eight members, "I would speak up." He frequently had to correct misinformation that worked its way into the report and he insisted on truthful terminology. Euphemisms like "evacuation," "relocation" (featured in the Commission's name), and "assembly center," sounded, to Marutani, "like we're going on a Boy Scout jamboree."[46]

The stated purposes of the Civil Liberties Act were to (1) acknowledge the fundamental injustice of incarceration; (2) apologize on behalf of "the people"—citizens, presumably, not the government—for incarceration; (3) provide for an education fund to inform the public about incarceration; (4) pay reparations to those who were incarcerated, including (5) the Indigenous Unangax (Aleut) people of the Aleutian Islands, approximately 800 of whom were forcibly removed to camps in southeastern Alaska; (6) "discourage the occurrence of similar injustices and violations of civil liberties in the future," "discourage" being a noncommittal way of putting it; and (7) "make more credible and sincere any declaration of concern by the United States over violations of human rights committed by other nations," deflecting responsibility away from itself and projecting it onto the rest of the world.

The Civil Liberties Public Education Fund was originally slated for $50 million, but was lobbied down to $5 million, $3.3 million of which went to public projects, including school curricula. The consequences of the fund being

---

46. William Marutani, interviewed by Becky Fukuda and Gary Kawaguchi, September 11, 1997, Densho Visual History Collection, Densho Digital Archive

gutted before final authorization is that, decades later—and, one could imagine, in perpetuity—people in the United States still graduate high school without knowing much, if anything, about Japanese American incarceration, the lackluster, perhaps illusory, paragraphs in US history textbooks notwithstanding.

The Civil Liberties Act was signed by Ronald Reagan, on August 10, 1988. In the photographs, Reagan looks, sitting at a wooden desk, surrounded by men, Japanese American and white, and one Japanese American woman, like a child learning to write his name. In one photograph, like he is painting a watercolor. In another, he is holding the pen triumphantly in the air, while everyone hovers around him, applauding.

One month before James Baldwin died, he was asked what he thought Reagan represented to white America. "Ronald Reagan represents the justification of their history, their sense of innocence," he replied. "The justification, in short, of being white."[47]

Here, in no particular order, are some of the components that facilitated the dispossession, forced removal, and mass incarceration of Japanese immigrants and Japanese Americans during WWII, amounting to a catalog of democracy in action: anti-immigrant propaganda; anti-immigrant legislation; dehumanizing rhetoric (the Japanese were bugs, dogs, lice, monkeys, rats, skunks, snakes); racial segregation; racial profiling; surveillance and the maintenance of secret databases; warrantless raids; media complicity in

47. James Baldwin, interviewed by Quincy Troupe, St. Paul de Vence, France, November 1987. In *The Last Interview and Other Conversations* (Brooklyn, NY: Melville House, 2014)

fomenting anxiety and rage; family separation; the devastation of families, family structures; the severing of people from their ancestry, their origins; the criminalization of language and culture; perpetual and arbitrary tests of loyalty and allegiance; forced submission to the ideologies and behaviors of national security citizenship; the dispossession and theft of property; forms of social control derived from penitentiaries, plantations, native reservations; the occupation of Indigenous land; exploitative labor; a Constitution so reliant upon interpretation, and so unequally applied, as to be completely subjective; an apology, which does not exist outside of a crime, but is part of it, fundamental to it: as an alibi, a transitioning of the crime into the realm of reconciliation, and an ushering of history into oblivion.[48]

---

48. The United States apologized for protecting Klaus Barbie, a Gestapo agent responsible for the deaths of 14,000 French prisoners during WWII. The United States enlisted Barbie for counterintelligence and coordinated his escape to South America. The apology came in 1983. The United States apologized for backing a coup, led by white businessmen, to overthrow Queen Lili'uokalani and the Kingdom of Hawai'i, in 1893. The apology came one hundred years later, in 1993. The United States apologized for the Tuskegee Experiment, in which 600 Black men from Alabama were enlisted in a syphilis study, but without their knowledge or consent. They were told they were being treated for "bad blood." Four hundred of the men had syphilis, 200 did not, but, despite the availability of penicillin, they were not treated, only given aspirin and vitamins. More than 100 of the men died. Others went blind or insane. Their wives contracted syphilis, as did their newborn babies. The study was to last six months, but lasted forty years. The apology came sixty-five years after the tests began, in 1997. The United States House of Representatives, not exactly the United States, apologized for the *"fundamental injustice, cruelty, brutality, and inhumanity"* of slavery and Jim Crow. The apology came in 2008 and cited, as an example, the apology for the "imprisonment of Japanese-Americans during World War II." Despite that, and despite expressing a commitment to "rectify the lingering consequences" of slavery, the apology denied the possibility of reparations. The United States apologized *for the "many instances" of violence inflicted on Native Peoples by citizens—as opposed, once again, to the government—of the United States.* The apology is buried in Section 8113 of the Department of Defense Appropriations Act of 2010. Apology, from the Greek *apologos*, meaning "story," consigns a transgression to the past, while expecting, more often

"Yes, we received an apology," said children's book author Maggie Tokuda-Hall, whose grandparents were in Minidoka, in an interview, "we even received reparations. But our government hasn't changed in a fundamental way, so I don't accept the apology."[49]

With the Civil Liberties Act, the United States closed the book on Japanese American incarceration, with the overbearing hand of both the proud, proprietary storyteller and the person who is tired of, more truthfully haunted by, the story. "Internment's haunting," writes Jessica Nakamura, in *Transgenerational Remembrance*, "suggests that legislative action does not end historiographical debates or relieve experiences of personal pain caused by unconstitutional, oppressive, or violent acts."

Actually, the United States did not close the book; it took a razor blade, cut out every word, and rearranged each one, in dreadfully predictable configurations, across the pages of twenty-first-century American existence. The Civil Liberties Act, masquerading as an act of reconciliation, was an act of control. It galvanized, out of voluminous testimony, a regeneration of silence.

In the darkness of ancient islands, the newly dead tasted the acid life of the coin. How much is $20,000 not worth? Reparations paid for one year of my grandfather's dying. I asked my grandmother about the check, if she remembered receiving it. She did not. I had to remind her what it was. She took a minute, rolled her lips. It did not arrive automatically, she said. Someone told her about it, she

demanding, forgiveness, in the present. It puts the burden of responsibility of historical closure on the victims, those still suffering, to forgive, accept their fate, shut up and move on.
49. *The Lead with Jake Tapper*, CNN, May 12, 2023

could not remember who. Somehow it arrived. But it did not inspire conversation. Any sense of vindication was personal, private. The check was deposited. The letter disappeared just as quickly.

SAVING THE INCENSE

"I REMEMBER A MEMORY. I REMEMBER THINKING I WAS old enough to have memories. I remember playing war with grandma. I remember her complaining about the lack of privacy. I remember seeing a photo of the bathrooms. I remember being aghast. I remember mom talking about *camp*. I remember thinking she had gone to *summer camp*. I remember her describing how the barracks were made. I remember mom talking about the wind blowing sand into the barracks. I remember how the camps changed her relationship with her identity. I remember telling her I thought she didn't speak Japanese and she laughed and said she didn't. I remember it was blazing hot. I remember driving around the reservation as the sun was setting. I remember the white monument in the cemetery. I remember a plaque. I remember thinking, *Is this it? Is this all that's left?* I remember being disappointed. I remember my father pointing out where some of the things would have been. I remember them pointed out on a map. I remember my mom pointing out people in a sea of names. I remember looking up my relatives' names in the roster. I remember searching for _____ . I remember getting out of the car. I remember how windy it was. I remember the hot wind whipping my hair. I remember looking at the fields. I remember the plants. I remember feeling like I was intruding. I remember a heaviness. I remember asking what internment meant. I remember asking a few times. I remember asking my sister. I remember never discussing it at school. I remember a small paragraph in my textbook. I remember a book report. I remember a very short assignment. I remember winning an award for the assignment. I remember looking conspicuous. I remember people did not believe the camps existed. I remember being angry. I remember the story about the wooden birds. I remember feeling like it wasn't my story to tell. I remember my grandmother saying they could only take what fit in two suitcases. I remember her telling me about answering *No No* on the questionnaire. I remember a relative who served in the 442nd. I remember bringing his medals to school. I remember grandpa was emotional. I remember grandmother was sad. I remember a kimono grandma had. I remember sitting in my grandparents' living room. I remember I had a list of questions. I remember being surprised at how matter-of-fact they were. I remember being confused because I had no context. I remember being ashamed. I remember not wanting to ask grandma to clarify. I remember hearing grandpa was jailed for being a spy. I remember mother justifying why. I remember asking my dad about propaganda. I remember seeing it on TV. I remember thinking why wasn't everyone watching? I remember being confused by the lack of engagement. I remember it feeling like it wasn't a big deal. I remember feeling disconnected. I remember my dad telling me to never identify my race on a form. I remember my father taking off his glasses. I remember him talking in his sleep. I remember hearing my mom and aunts and grandpa talk about reparations. I remember my grandparents receiving a check in the mail. I remember being angry at the government because the check arrived late. I remember my parents showing me the check. I remember my mom explaining what it was. I remember when grandma got the letter from the president. I remember seeing the letter. I remember my father valuing the apology more than the money. I remember he would point to the letter on the wall. I remember mom saying she wished her parents were still alive. I remember grandmother launching small paper boats. I remember watching grandfather light incense. I remember thinking is this something I'm supposed to do? I remember feeling awe and relief. I remember the smell. I remember saving the incense."

SUNKEN ROOMS

"WE WERE INSTRUCTED TO PULL THE SHADES DOWN," A young girl told me, about the train rides from the detention centers to the concentration camps. "They did not want us to see where we were. They did not want us to see where we were going." Even if they could, they would not have known where that was. They were being ferried beyond forgetting into bleached outer space. And were becoming, under the watchful yet dispassionate eyes of America, migrants—unwitting, non-consensual migrants—whose destination was not a place but a condition. Not only did they not know where they were going, they did not know how long it would take to get there, or how long they were going to stay. They were being separated from one reality and forced into another. "Because it is psychotic not to know where you are in a national space," writes Bhanu Kapil in *Schizophrene*. The shades pulled down the windows became portraits of each individual as they stared into the reflection of their apprehension—for some, the young, their adventure—slipping into the darkness of America. As if their fate was not what awaited them in that landscape, but their own faces staring back.

I met the young girl in the Japanese American Museum of San Jose, California. She greeted me at the entrance, asked if I wanted a tour. As we entered the exhibition, she told me a story.

"Don't get too close to the ditches, the older boys said," she began. "If you do, snapping turtles will grab you and pull you in." It was her first day in the desert. Her first hour. The desert, except for a few hills that looked like they were hiding something, was flat. The young girl would grow familiar with, knowledgeable about, maybe even fall in love with the desert. She was there because she was put there. By her country. Which looked at her, or did not look at her, and determined that she was their enemy. Which meant also that she was her own enemy, but what did that mean?

She thought of hundreds, thousands, of snapping turtles, waiting, at the bottoms of ditches, with yellow eyes like squash and green eyes like zucchini. This is how you become a snapping turtle, she thought, this is how you stop being a human and become a snapping turtle. But how do you become an enemy? Maybe love is the feeling of being familiar with and knowledgeable about a person or place you are forced to be in relation with *indefinitely.* The young girl looked at the desert, the hills that looked like they were hiding something, then the barbed wire, a guard tower looming above it, a man whose face was partly obscured by the gun that was aimed at *her* face.

It was her face, after all, that inspired the invention of the camps. She pointed to a black-and-white photograph on the wall. It showed, from the vantage of a hill, maybe a guard tower, rows of military barracks. The photograph was bright, almost blinding. Its subject seemed to be, in one sense, the sun. It looked like it was promoting a housing development, which is one way the camps were propagandized: as "pioneer communities."[50] "You are the new pioneers," said Ralph

---

50. "In fact," writes Vince Schleitwiler, in Apparitions of the Non-Alien: Manzanar, "one initial idea was to house the entire population in a single place—an all-Japanese American prison city hidden in the mountains!"

Merritt, director of Manzanar, in a speech to high school students. Pioneer, from the French *pionnier*, meaning "foot soldier," from the Latin *pedo*, meaning "pawn."

"We used to dig holes beneath the barracks to stay cool," the young girl said, pointing at one of the barracks. "We cut holes in the floors"—under tables, beneath beds, behind dressers—"and built sunken rooms." The metaphors of being forced underground, into hiding, and being forced to dig one's own grave, came to mind, and I wondered if these metaphors came to the minds of the people as they sat in the holes.

In Gila River, to escape the 100 degree heat, people slept in the holes. Gambled, played dice, cards, hanafuda. In his archeological study of Gila River, Koji Lau-Ozawa describes a raid on one of the holes that turned up "1½ gallons of raison jack, 1 quart of sake and a barrel with 35 gallons of sake mash fermenting."[51] Mamoru Eto, the first to receive reparations, dug a hole beneath his barracks in Gila River and converted it into a den, where he wrote sermons and shigin poetry. George Hirahara and his son Frank dug a hole beneath their barracks in Heart Mountain and converted it into a darkroom, half photo developing lab, half portrait studio. There was a trapdoor beneath their dining table with stairs going down. They ordered cameras and equipment from Sears Roebuck and Montgomery Ward catalogs. A refrigerator was sent from Yakima, "to keep the film and chemicals cool." They kept another trapdoor open at night to let out the fumes.

Growing up, Frank's daughter, Patti Hirahara, did not know about the darkroom. Neither her father nor her grandfather talked about it until she started to ask questions. "I think they were worried that it might come back

---

51. Koji Lau-Ozawa, Japanese Diaspora in a WWII Incarceration Camp: Archaeology of Gila River

to haunt them," Patti told me. "I think my grandfather still worried his family might get into trouble. But they knew they were recording history and that their photos would be invaluable someday."

While moving her grandparents from Yakima to the Keiro Nursing Home, Patti found a box in their attic labeled "Heart Mountain." Inside were 850 negatives. Eighteen years later, she found 1,200 more negatives in her father's closet.[52] Photographs of life in camp, school days at Heart Mountain High School (where Frank was a student, photo editor of the yearbook, and Associated Student Body Commissioner of General Activities), class pictures, graduations, weddings, Obon. Many of the photographs are of babies: Baby Nakamura in a dress next to an inflatable deer; Babies Hori and Yonemura holding rattles; Babies Sumida, Oba, Hanafusa, and Toshibomi on plaid blankets. A crying baby was photographed on August 12, 1945. Another crying baby was photographed also on August 12. On August 13, "Baby Matsumoto on a blanket." Also on August 13, "Little girl on a box." On August 15, Hirohito addressed Japan, his voice emanating, posthumous and unreal, through every speaker in the nation. "宜シク擧國一家、子孫相傳ヘ、確ク神州ノ不滅ヲ信シ、任重クシテ道遠キヲ念ヒ、總力ヲ將來ノ建設ニ傾ケ、道義ヲ篤クシ、志操ヲ鞏クシ、誓テ國體ノ精華ヲ發揚シ、世界ノ進運ニ後レサラムコトヲ期スヘシ。" On August 28, day one of the US occupation of Japan, several photographs were taken of ikebana on cloth-covered shelves in a barrack. On August 29, Baby Motoyoshi with a stuffed dog.

Roy Higa was fourteen when he dug a basement beneath the barracks he shared with his parents. "It gets very hot at Manzanar, very windy, and in the summertime, there's

52. She donated them to the Yakima Valley Museum and Washington State University. They are available to view online at the George and Frank C. Hirahara Photograph Collection, 1943–1945, WSU Libraries Digital Collections: content.libraries.wsu.edu/digital/collection/hiraharag

nothing much you can do," Higa said in an interview.[53]
"Since I grew up in a nursery, I like to dig." It took three
days. He spread the dirt around the block, sometimes in
people's gardens. The basement was five feet deep, five feet
square, trapdoor, three steps down. He made a table from
scrap lumber and chairs out of crates from the mess hall,
so that he and his friends could play cards. He watered the
walls to keep the heat down.

In July 2015, the National Park Service organized an
excavation of Roy's basement, as part of an archeological survey of the block where Roy's family lived. His son
Mitchell took part. The first time Mitchell visited Manzanar, in the 1980s, there was little signage, no visitor center. "The camp seemed desolate, abandoned." Mitchell told
me. "I had to drive aimlessly around to find the cemetery."

The excavation took five days. They used a map Roy had
drawn from memory. "It was remarkably accurate to within
a foot or two," Mitchell told me. "We had to do everything
very carefully. We couldn't just go in there with a backhoe
and rip the ground apart. Everything was done by hand." [54]
Mitchell called his father to tell him how the dig was going.
Roy was excited that they found his basement, but disappointed that the table and chairs were not there.

After Roy and his family were moved from Manzanar
to Tule Lake, "somebody else expanded my dad's basement," Mitchell said. "And then when the camp closed, it
became a landfill. Until we came along, seventy years later,
to dig it up."

The basement might have looked, from above, like the
footprint of a very small house. Or an evacuated grave. "It
was like discovering a shallow grave," said Warren Furutani
about visiting Manzanar in 1969, "where the elements had

53. Roy Higa, interviewed by Laura Ng, July 2, 2012, Manzanar National
Historic Site
54. Mitchell Higa, interviewed by Amanda Tewes, Oral History Center,
Bancroft Library, UC Berkeley, 2022

blown the top layer off, and then the grave was exposed, and you could see a whole history."[55]

The sunken rooms—"gestures of rebellion and autonomy," writes Neil Nakadate in *Looking After Minidoka*—were banned in the summer of 1943 "for the benefit of the residents," because of "cave-ins, water seepage, unsanitary conditions."[56]

My earliest imagination of what the barracks looked like was the widow's hut in Hiroshi Teshigahara's film 砂の女, *Woman in the Dunes*: sunken, lost to the world, and concealing, beneath the accumulating drifts, the bodies of family members who had been waiting, with desperate faith, to be found, and a desperate feeling that they would never be found. Everything would be covered in dust, the overgrowth of time and abandonment. But the dust prefigured an even more complicated truth: that the camps, newly and poorly built, were *already* ruins, were already blowing away.

Dust enters
during the night like a thief
leaving mounds
of sand in all corners
of the room where the wind left it.[57]

that unending wind
drowning prisoners in dust.[58]

55. Quoted in Karen M. Inouye, *The Long Afterlife of Nikkei Wartime Incarceration.* (Stanford, CA: Stanford University Press, 2016)
56. Manzanar visitor center
57. Mariko Nagai, "October 1942," *Dust of Eden* (Park Ridge, IL: Albert Whitman & Company, 2014)
58. Amy Uyematsu, "36 Views of Manzanar," *The Blue Trickster Time* (Topanga, CA: What Books Press, 2022)

How many times have we made life from dust?[59]

My grandfather's tongue
lay caked in dust.[60]

The desert—all dust—
                    dammed Pa's mouth.[61]

But what we don't anticipate
is how the dust of the desert will clot our throats.[62]

The mouth and its silent
dust.[63]

At the end of the tour, the young girl led me into a room at the back of the museum: a reconstructed barrack, wood walls and floors, exposed ceiling, cots, tables, chairs. I had been there before, in similar reconstructions in other museums—at Fort Missoula, Topaz, Manzanar, the Japanese American National Museum.

When Gail Montgomery and her mother, Kazue Nishimoto Kudo, visited the barrack at JANM, Montgomery was overwhelmed, "sobbing," she said, while her mother [who was in Santa Anita and Manzanar] said, "Ours weren't this nice. We nailed tin can lids over the knotholes to keep the dust out."

When Corinne Araki-Kawaguchi visited the barrack at JANM, she noticed the spaces between the slats in the

59. Mia Ayumi Malhotra, "Sheltering," *Isako Isako* (New Gloucester, ME: Alice James Books, 2018)

60. W. Todd Kaneko, "Legacies of Camp," *This is How the Bone Sings* (Mount Vernon, NY: Black Lawrence Press, 2020)

61. Sharon Hashimoto, "A Barrack's Window, Inside," *More American* (Beacon, NY: Grid Books, 2021)

62. Christine Kitano, "Gaman," *Sky Country* (Rochester, NY: BOA Editions Ltd, 2017)

63. Brian Komei Dempster, "Truce," *Seize* (New York: Four Way Books, 2020)

wall. "I remember mom [who was in Gila River] talking about the wind blowing sand in," she said. "She had to constantly sweep the sand out. It must have seemed like an endless battle. She hid her makeup, lest her lipstick picked up the grit."

When Dylan Fujioka visited the barrack at JANM, he was amazed at how small it was. "I pictured myself living inside," he said. "That was the first time I truly understood that the incarceration was real. It wasn't just a story my mom [whose father was in Tule Lake] was telling me."

When my sister, Kelly Shimoda, visited the barrack at JANM, she thought about "how much mental and emotional strength it must have taken" to dismantle it and relocate it to the museum. "I wondered if it was therapeutic, tearing them down," she said, "and how it felt for whomever rebuilt it."

When Chelsea Fujimoto visited the barrack at JANM, she "stood for a long while in front of the quote on the back wall: *I went to Heart Mountain to tear down some walls. Now I gently embrace them.*" Being there was "like a sucker punch to the gut." She had thirteen family members in camp—Manzanar, Minidoka, Poston, Rohwer, Tule Lake. She thought of her grandmother, "like feeling her spirit in the walls."

"I recall touching the barrack wall," said Sumi Araki Kawaguchi, Corinne's daughter, "and drawing the emotion out."

When Erin Aoyama visited the barrack at Heart Mountain, where her grandmother Misa was incarcerated, she noticed, on the cot, a knitted blanket, the kind her grandmother was always knitting, many of which Aoyama had in her house growing up. When she saw it, she felt, as she told me, "yanked out of my body."

"Is this what it felt like?" I asked the young girl.

"This is what it felt like," she said. Then she said: "This is what it feels like."

The young girl was, when I met her, eighty-two. Yoshiko Kanazawa was six when she was incarcerated in Santa Anita then Gila River. She told me it had taken her entire life to tell her story. That, motivated by the passing of survivors, more pointedly by the inflammation of anti-Muslim racism, she began telling her story—to her church, to elementary school students, to people she walked with through the museum. After we said goodbye, she became, in my memory, a young girl—appealing to her elder self for guidance, the elder appealing to her younger self for redemption.

I walked down 5th Street to Jackson. Between the sidewalk and the street were five benches that looked, in their haphazard arrangement, like they had been unloaded very quickly from a truck. They were inscribed with the names of the camps and faced, at odd angles, the same sculpture with bas-relief panels that stands in Japantown in San Francisco and Los Angeles. Hammered onto a utility pole was a reproduction in pressed metal of INSTRUCTIONS TO ALL PERSONS OF JAPANESE ANCESTRY. Beneath it, a flyer: MISSING CAT.

The benches were covered in pink and white magnolia petals. I thought of the old man in Sawako Ariyoshi's *The Twilight Years* gazing up at the magnolia in the rain: "Perhaps he had been drawn to its beauty because he instinctively sensed the approach of death."[64] I imagined people appearing each night to sit together on the benches, catch up and keep each other company. And then, as the sun touched the roof of the church across the street, disappearing.

---

64. Sawako Ariyoshi, *The Twilight Years*, translated from the Japanese by Mildred Tahara

How many memorials are oriented towards the dead, are made with the dead in mind? Not to educate or instruct the living, not to invite the living's contemplation of history, but to provide a space for the dead to come together and be with each other again?

Years later, when I visited the benches—I missed them, and was not sure if I had made up the detail about them being haphazard—a funeral procession was coming down 5th. Norm Mineta had just died. Lisa, Yumi, and I were in Nichi Bei Bussan, the department store run by the Tatsuno family. It had been in business for 120 years. Arlene had taken it over from her father, Dave (whose camera was behind glass in the Topaz Museum), who had taken it over from his father, Shojiro. I was not entirely sure where the store ended and the family's personal belongings began. Arlene told me the procession was coming, did we want to go? But first, she said, let me show you something. She opened a glass display case and pulled out a phone book from 1968 that listed every Japanese and Japanese American person and business in the United States, from the Pacific to the Mississippi. There was my great-uncle Yoshio Shimoda on East Washington Boulevard in Whittier, my great-uncle Makio Shimoda on South 6th Street in Salt Lake City, my great-uncle Harry Yamashita on Grant Avenue in Ogden.

Mineta—his ashes—was carried in a black limousine. Fourteen cops on motorcycles rode in front. Black SUVs followed. People waved small American flags. A woman shook pompoms. A man in a yellow reflective vest rode a hoverboard in front of the limo. The procession stopped in front of Wesley United Methodist Church. The congregation sang "Go Now in Peace," but I could not see anyone's mouth moving. The windows of the limo were down. A white woman in the far back was waving. Mineta's wife, maybe, or the Coast Guard carrying his ashes. Two older men held an enormous flag, the stripes covered in signatures. Even though American politics could not be separated from overwrought displays of violence masquerading as patriotism and peace-keeping, the cops with their gourd-like heads above the whirling lights were incongruous and excessive, offending what should have been the solemn floating of the ashes down the silent sea of people.

The swamp was still. I was the only one on the train. Along the platform at the end of the yellow line stood three large torii, a fourth and fifth before an enormous parking lot. The torii were made of gray wood. Wrapped around their posts were reproductions in pressed metal of the front pages of local newspapers from 1942: "Portland to Be First Jap-Free City: Next Tuesday to Find Town Sans Nippos"; "Japs Hasten to Register in Portland"; "Big Pavilion to Receive 4,000 Japs." Metal ID tags hung from ropes along the beams. Blank, no names. *Voices of Remembrance*: an installation by the artist Valerie Otani.

I walked through the torii into the parking lot. A white man was blowing leaves. He turned off his blower.

"Can I help you?" he asked, suspicious.

"Do you know these buildings very well?" I answered, suspiciously.

"Why, what are you looking for?"

"A plaque."

The leaves scattered. "I think I know which one," he said, behaving, suddenly, like he had been waiting for me. "It's inside A Hall." He pointed to a building set back from a newer, fancier building. "It's closed, but I can take you."

Ron. We walked across the parking lot and entered a warehouse. The concrete floors gleamed. I thought of the cavernous room filled with mounds of sand in Andrei Tarkovsky's *Stalker*. Ron took me to a carpeted lobby. Mounted on a brick wall above a bench between two fake plants and beneath a wide-screen TV was a plaque that detailed, very briefly, the incarceration, in that spot, of Japanese Americans, May 2 to September 10, 1942. It was illustrated with a sun rising above clouds, barbed wire across the text. (Kodansha: 1987)

The Portland Expo Center, formerly the Pacific International Livestock and Exhibition Center, transformed, in the spring of 1942, into a detention center where 3,676 Japanese immigrants and Japanese Americans from Oregon and Washington were incarcerated before being sent to Minidoka and Heart Mountain. I tried to resurrect the sound of thousands of people, harried, exhausted, turning down into night, the building creaking under the weight of the transformation of a community into a prison population, but I could only conjure a mass of white Americans (Portland is 75% white) pushing, gelatinously, through the halls to see wedding dresses or boats or Cirque du Soleil, every once in a while someone catching sight of something flickering high on the wall, their eyes just grazing the plaque.

The plaque was lonely, pathetic.[65] A formality, begrudging. Ron seemed to have some feeling for it though. He stood next to me, looked up at the plaque. He was still wearing the blower. He looked like he was trying his best to absorb, more plainly decode, the little the plaque had to share. He looked at me, with an expression that said, *Is that you?* "My family wasn't here," I said. "Okay then, I'll leave you alone."

Where did Ron go? The tags in the wind sounded like bells, people putting on bells for a festival. Not like an element in a modest retrospective of dark history, but of life going on just beyond what was visible. Maybe the true intention of

---

65. "I love plaques," Erin Aoyama told me. "They say a lot more about whoever put them up than what actually happened there."

the memorial was to lure the visitor to the end of the line, into the swamp, to distract them, so that the people who were being commemorated could carry on, out of sight, a more personal memorial elsewhere.

I rode the train back into Portland, to visit the Japanese American Historical Plaza. I was again the only person. A white bird hovered over a swamp. It reminded me of train rides I had taken through rural Japan, small towns like ellipses, the doors opening onto platforms overgrowing with weeds, no one getting on or off. There were always rice fields just beyond the platform, and always, in each rice field, a white egret.

JAPANESE AMERICAN
HISTORICAL PLAZA

THE FIRST TIME I VISITED THE JAPANESE AMERICAN HIS-torical Plaza in Portland, Oregon, a young girl and a middle-aged woman were chasing each other through the cherry trees. They made no sound. The girl stopped beneath the trees and stared across the river. Then she began to scream. Her scream rose into the trees, raced to the ends of their limbs. The woman began signing to the girl. The girl stared at the woman, her hands, then ran out of the trees and behind the tall stone in the center of the plaza. Inscribed on the stone were ten names:

Gila
Granada
Heart Mountain
Jerome
Manzanar
Minidoka
Poston
Rohwer
Topaz
Tule Lake

I wondered how tall the stone would have to be to carry

not only the names of the ten concentration camps, but the names of all the detention centers and prisons and internment camps and labor camps and isolation centers and immigration stations and jails and hotels and hospitals where Japanese immigrants and Japanese Americans were incarcerated during WWII:

Alum Rock Sanitarium, CA
Amache concentration camp, CO
Annette Island Land Field, AK
Arroyo Del Valle Sanitarium, CA
Asheville Grove Park Inn, NC
Bedford Springs Hotel, PA
Bret Harte Sanatorium, CA
Camarillo State Hospital, CA
Camp Algiers internment camp, LA
Camp Forrest internment camp, TN
Camp Livingston internment camp, LA
Camp McCoy internment camp, WI
Camp Upton, NY
Chatham County Jail, GA
Chicago INS detention station, IL
Cincinnati INS detention station, OH
Cow Creek, CA
Crystal City internment camp, TX
Dallas INS detention station, TX
East Boston INS detention station, MA
Ellis Island detention station, NY
Fort Bliss internment camp, TX
Fort Crook internment camp, NE
Fort Howard internment camp, MD
Fort Leavenworth US disciplinary barracks, KS
Fort Leonard Wood, MO
Fort Lewis internment camp, WA
Fort Lincoln internment camp, ND
Fort McDowell (Angel Island) internment camp, CA

Fort Meade internment camp, MD
Fort Missoula internment camp, MT
Fort Omaha, NE
Fort Richardson internment camp, AK
Fort Sam Houston internment camp, TX
Fort Sill internment camp, OK
Fort Stanton segregation camp, NM
Fresno detention center, CA
Galveston INS detention station, TX
Gila River concentration camp, AZ
Glouchester City INS station, NJ
Greenbrier Hotel, WV
Griffith Park detention station, CA
Haiku camp, HI
Harris County jail, TX
Hartford INS detention station, CT
Heart Mountain concentration camp, WY
Hillcrest Sanitorium, CA
Hilo Independent Language School, HI
Honolulu INS administration building, HI
Honouliuli internment camp, HI
Hot Springs Homestead Hotel, VA
Jerome concentration camp, AR
Kalaheo Stockade, HI
Kenedy internment camp, TX
Kern County Jail, CA
Kilauea military camp, HI
Kings County Hospital, CA
Kooskia internment camp, ID
Lanai City Jail, HI
Leupp isolation center, AZ
Lordsburg internment camp, NM
Los Angeles County Jail, CA
Los Angeles General Hospital, CA
Manzanar concentration camp, CA
Maryknoll Sanitarium, CA

Marysville (Arboga) detention center, CA
Mayer detention center, AZ
McNeill Island penitentiary, WA
Merced County Hospital, CA
Merced County Jail, CA
Merced detention center, CA
Miami police station, FL
Minidoka concentration camp, ID
Moab isolation center, UT
Montreat Assembly Inn, NC
New Jersey Police Department Long Branch, NJ
Nyssa tent camp, OR
Old Raton Ranch internment camp, NM
Olive View Sanitorium, CA
Orange County Jail, CA
Owens Valley reception center, CA
Pacific Colony, CA
Parker Dam reception center, CA
Patton State Hospital, CA
Phoenix Desmount Sanatorium, AZ
Pinedale detention center, CA
Pomona detention center, CA
Port Arthur City Jail, TX
Portland detention center, OR
Poston concentration camp, AZ
Puyallup detention center, WA
Rohwer concentration camp, AR
Sacramento (Walerga) detention center, CA
Salinas detention center, CA
Salt Lake City INS station, UT
Salt Lake City Jail, UT
Salt Lake County Jail, UT
San Diego County Hospital, CA
San Diego County Jail, CA
San Francisco County Hospital, CA
San Francisco INS detention station, CA

San Joaquin County Jail, CA
San Jose City Jail, CA
San Pedro INS detention station, CA
Sand Island internment camp, HI
Santa Ana City Jail, CA
Santa Anita detention center, CA
Santa Anita Sanitarium, CA
Santa Barbara County Jail, CA
Santa Fe internment camp, NM
Seagoville internment camp, TX
Seattle Firland Sanatorium, WA
Seattle INS detention station, WA
Sharp Park detention station, CA
South End Community House, CT
Spokane County Jail, WA
Stamford City Jail, CT
Stockton detention center, CA
Tacoma City Jail, WA
Tanforan detention center, CA
Topaz concentration camp, UT
Trudeau Sanatorium, NY
Tucson Federal Prison, AZ
Tulare detention center, CA
Tulare-Kings Counties Joint Tuberculosis Hospital, CA
Tule Lake concentration camp, CA
Tuna Canyon detention station, CA
Turlock detention center, CA
Utah State Mental Hospital, UT
Vauclain Home, CA
Ventura County Jail, CA
Wailua County Jail, HI
Wailuku County Jail, HI
Weimar Sanitarium, CA
White Pine County Jail, NV
Wish-I-Ah Sanitorium, CA

I SEE THE MEMORY OUTLINE

If you have not visited the site or sites where your family members were incarcerated, what do you imagine the site or sites (places, landscapes) look and feel like?[66]

"Desolate," said Mia Ayumi Malhotra.

"Empty, lonely, desolate," said Brad Shirakawa.

"Sad, dry, desolate," said Danielle Steckler.

"Cold, dry, crumbling, desolate," said Deborah Cristobal.

"Hollow and sunken, cold and dry and desolate," said Kai Sase Ebens.

"Barren, windswept, and desolate," said Julie Yamamoto.

"Dry, brushy, and windswept," said Sesshu Foster.

"I imagine them haunted—windswept," Mia Ayumi Malhotra continued.

"I feel they must be haunted," said Starr Miyata.

"I fear it would feel too haunting," said Jessica Kashiwabara.

---

66. Some of the people quoted in this chapter have, since the writing of this book, visited the sites they were imagining, and would likely have something different to say about what they saw, what they thought, and how it felt to be there.

"I imagine feeling haunted and suffocated," said Erin Tsutsumoto.

"I imagine that they feel both hollow and haunted," said Casey Hidekawa Lane/Levinski. "Like a grave with no body."

"In my imagination, I see dust, desert, mountains, stones," said Brynn Saito.

"Possibly with mountains visible in the distance," said Evan Iwata.

"With mountains and forests in the distance," said Dylan Mori.

"Those mountains have seen everything," said Liana Hisako Tai.

"I imagine the camps to be hot, dry, uncomfortable, dusty," said Dylan Fujioka.

"I imagine the site is destitute, bleak, dusty," said Lauryn Takisaki.

"I imagine it's barren, hot, dusty," said Gail Montgomery.

"Dust howling across empty land," Mia Ayumi Malhotra continued.

"Because all I can remember from my grandmother's stories is that there was sand everywhere," said Anna Kimura, "and that the wind would blow the sand into every crevice."

"I imagine dust and sun and some kind of emptiness and disappointment," said Fred Sasaki, "like finding some vacant part of me."

"I imagine the quiet, and the wind kicking up dust, and relics of these hastily built, falling-apart places," said Chelsea Fujimoto.

"I imagine it feels rather bleak," said Alyxandra Reed-Asakawa.

"Bleak, barren, and void of historical markers beyond perhaps a token sign or two," said Jenna Nishimura.

"Bleak and isolated," said Jennifer Mie Oda, "with trauma embedded in the existing buildings and surrounding landscape."

"I imagine that there are still traces of the site," said Christina Hiromi Hobbs, "maybe the remnants of barracks, or scraps of furniture or clothes that were left behind."

"I imagine that most of the buildings and structures have fallen down," said Rebekah Wada.

"I imagine most places have been torn down and destroyed," said Leigh Ann Tomooka, "because why would the US want to highlight such a stain."

"I imagine that the site of the camp is almost completely erased as if it never existed," Christina Hiromi Hobbs continued.

"My fear," said Megan Kowta, "is that it might feel as though it never happened."

"I imagine them as dead places," Chelsea Fujimoto continued.

"I imagine them as ghost towns," said Aaron Caycedo-Kimura.

"A ghost town with trees and grass filling in the spaces where people used to be," said Kristin Kamoto.

"A bit like a ghost town, a bit like a museum," Dylan Mori continued.

"I'd imagine the site feels like a monastery," said Matthew Kenichi Muranaga. "An atmospheric vessel for the lives and histories of generations lost."

"I imagine that wandering around the site would be a ghostly experience," Christina Hiromi Hobbs continued.

"I think I would feel overwhelmed by the ghosts," said Madeleine Mori, "but I do plan to let them speak to me some day."

"Maybe I would feel closer to my ancestors," Christina Hiromi Hobbs continued.

"I think I would feel the intensity and sorrow from the land," said Miya Sommers.

"I would probably be consumed with rage and pain," said Viki Yamashita. "This anger would be in addition to the fact that these centers of oppression would be built on stolen land."

"I think I would feel overwhelming grief and loneliness," said Yoshiko Yeto, "but somehow marvel at the stark beauty of this sacred Native American land."

"I imagine there is a way that the landscapes might actually be very beautiful," Starr Miyata continued.

"Lonely and desolate yet beautiful," said Maureen Poon Fear.

"Beautiful," said Kimiko Guthrie. "Lush. Wet. Green. Teeming with screaming insects, snakes, moss, woods, all forms of abundant, fertile life. But. The white supremacy lingering there—the barbed wire fences, the guard towers, the guards, the guns, the barracks, the fear—haunt the air in my mind. I see the memory outline of all that."

"I feel a sad and heavy heart when I think of what it looks like," said Tiffani Koyano.

"I can imagine feeling sad and confused," said Derek Inouye.

"I suspect I will feel angry and lost," Fred Sasaki continued.

"I think being there must be heartbreaking," said Lyn Ishizaki-Brown.

"I think it would depress me," said Debbi Michiko Florence.

"I think I'm just too scared," Kimiko Guthrie continued. "I feel a physical and emotional block to going. I feel a sickness in my stomach about being there. A repulsion. Maybe I feel, at some level, like *we escaped, why go back*? I think at some level I feel an irrational fear of being caught there. Not like time traveling and finding myself imprisoned, but I sense the ghost of barbed wire still there in the air that might snag me."

"I'm most interested in the sound of the place too," said Lois Harada.

JAPANESE AMERICAN
HISTORICAL PLAZA

THE SECOND TIME I VISITED THE JAPANESE AMERICAN Historical Plaza, two police officers, male, white, were harassing unhoused people. They had driven—screamed— their patrol car up over the curb and into the park and had stopped only a few feet from the people on the grass. They angled their car to block the people from getting past, climbed out with the menacing slowness of robots coming into possession of their faculties, and walked right into the people. They stood with their hands on their tasers and guns. There was no indication, anywhere in the park, that the people were in violation of any law. It was not until the police, and the fat bullet of their car, shot into the grass, that the peace had been disturbed.

Everything that belonged to the people—their backpacks and sleeping bags, their books, their dogs—belonged, in that moment, to the police, or so the police seemed to believe. They touched and tore into everything with violent disregard. I thought of the FBI agents invading and ransacking the homes of Japanese American families, how everything that the families did not have time to sell or give away or hide or burn or bury became vulnerable to the FBI. That is why the FBI was there: to criminalize anything they willfully misperceived as evidence that the

Japanese immigrants and their children and grandchildren were a threat to who and what they were protecting—white people, their property. The police scattered the people's belongings, then watched as the people scrambled to put everything back together. They made a show of watching every person as they walked out of the park, under the weight of more than they could reasonably carry.

According to a sign not far from this scene—written by Robert Murase, who was incarcerated as a young child in Tanforan and Topaz—the Japanese American Historical Plaza is "dedicated to helping people recognize and remember how precious constitutional civil liberties are, and how serious are the consequences when these basic freedoms are forsaken." But the mission seemed to be contradicted by the aggression that was being played out by the police. The Japanese American Historical Plaza was not guarding against such displays of force. It was inviting a brutal distinction to be made between people who should be left undisturbed and people who could be disturbed with impunity. What were the police doing if not enforcing an exclusion zone?

The task and the priority of any memorial to Japanese American incarceration must be the protection of the people who are at greatest risk of having their "civil liberties" and "basic freedoms" rejected, trodden upon and crushed, then and now. Which means that the only legitimate and the only honorable memorial to Japanese American incarceration is one in which no law enforcement, of any kind, would ever be permitted.

STATE OF ERASURE

THE MORNING DONALD TRUMP WAS INSTALLED AS THE 45th president of the United States, I was at the Holocaust History Center in Tucson. Robert Yerachmiel Sniderman, poet, artist, and program specialist at the museum, invited me to give a talk, which I used as an occasion to redress what I felt was Arizona's peculiar and persistent absence from the general narrative of Japanese American incarceration. There seemed to be little awareness, including among people in Tucson, that southern Arizona had been within the exclusion zone; that a line had been drawn east-west through Phoenix, and that every person of Japanese ancestry south of the line to the Mexican border was forced from their home and incarcerated; that Arizona had two of the largest camps—Poston and Gila River, both of which occupied Native reservations; that there were five other sites in Arizona in which Japanese nationals, Japanese immigrants and Japanese Americans were incarcerated; and that one of the sites, a federal prison labor camp, was on the mountain just north of us.

The ruins of these incarceration sites—marked or not, maintained or left to decay—were the prelude to the incarceration sites that were surrounding us in the present. Southeast of the Holocaust History Center, on South Wilmot, was

Tucson's Federal Correctional Institution. South of that, also on South Wilmot, was the US Penitentiary. South of that, also on South Wilmot, was Arizona State Prison. Southwest of the Holocaust History Center, on Silverlake, was the Pima County Prison. South of the Holocaust History Center, on Ajo, was the Pima County Juvenile Prison, which was, at the time, being considered for use as a child migrant detention center. North of the Holocaust History Center, on Oracle, in an old motel, palm trees peeking above the roof, was Southwest Key, an active child migrant detention center. "My dear, if it is not a city, it is a prison," writes Tongo Eisen-Martin, in his poem "Faceless." "If it has a prison, it is a prison. Not a city."[67]

Two days before the talk, I was advised by the museum not to mention Trump. I was confused. The transformation of the specter into reality was the day's occasion. The invitation, attested to by the existence of the museum and its focus on the history of genocide, was a prompt to talk about what was old and ingrained about what felt terrifyingly new. Trump's campaign, election, and now, his inauguration, were forcing an examination of what we did not know or refused knowing about our nation's foundational character, of which the new regime was the latest and most demonstrative iteration. I was not planning on mentioning Trump. His policy proposals were lifted, in sound and meaning, from the policies that formalized and enforced incarceration. His platform was to follow in the tradition of subjugation, dehumanization, and exclusion of non-white immigrants, citizens, and communities. Trump had already made himself ubiquitous. Inauguration Day was the confirmation of the misery.

"One way to make sense of Inauguration Day," I began, "is to acknowledge the word within the word: *augur*, to foretell events by interpreting omens. Some say *augur*

---

67. Tongo Eisen-Martin, "Faceless," *Heaven Is All Goodbyes* (San Francisco, CA: City Lights, 2017)

comes from the Latin for bird, and that the definition comes from the foretelling of events by interpreting the entrails of dead birds, more specifically, the entrails of birds that have been sacrificed. Inauguration Day, therefore, is a day to see, through the entrails harvested by sacrifice, what is to come, all the entrails re/constituting what has been, much of which has not yet been digested."[68]

The talk was followed by a Q&A. The first question was about daily life in Gila River. It felt anthropological, like we were on a field trip. A woman in the audience stood up. "There are people here who were there," she said, "ask them!" A man stood up and walked to the microphone. He looked like he was approaching a funeral dais. He stood before us but seemed to shrink into himself. His story was brief and said nothing about daily life in Gila River. He was not, despite the woman's injunction, there. He talked instead about his grandfather, who was there, but in vague, faraway terms. "My grandfather was a broken man," he said. He did not mention his grandfather's name, where he was born, when he immigrated to the United States, where he was when he was picked up by the FBI, or why, or if he was, or where he was incarcerated before Gila River. He had never met his grandfather, who died before he was born. He ended his story by saying, "but I've had success," as if his success was the necessary step in putting his grandfather back together, but he did not say anything about what he achieved. Maybe it did not matter. "Success" seemed to be a euphemism for having overcome history, or the belief that history could be overcome. I heard, in the negative space of the man's story, the shame of survival, and I felt the acid presence of the American Dream.

---

68. The full text of the talk is at *The Margins*, at the Asian American Writers' Workshop: aaww.org/state-erasure-arizona

And yet maybe what the man shared, the little he shared, was more illuminating than if he had simply answered the question about daily life in Gila River, because he was embodying the more pressing reality of the distance that was produced between generations.

Daily life in Gila River. People had sex in fields of silverleaf tomato weed and creosote poppies. Babies were born, babies died, babies cried, would not stop crying, a man anesthetized babies with lullabies. A reverend ran a lullaby workshop. A woman cooked meals for a cricket, had dreams of the cricket turning into a man. A cicada sang songs, people flocked to a unicorn mantis for advice. On the hottest day, newspapers caught fire, vats of wine exploded. People dug trenches beneath their barracks to "wait out the hottest portions of the day in the cooling shade," pooped through wooden planks over trenches, suffered hysteria, saw apparitions in the form of enormous moths. A woman and a man built a flying machine powered by ten thousand birds. A man with raven's black wings flew over the fence to smuggle whiskey into camp.

"My grandfather used to joke that he wanted me to write his memoir," Kiik Araki-Kawaguchi told me. He took his grandfather up on the joke and wrote it as fiction. *The Book of Kane and Margaret*, in which everything detailed in the above paragraph takes place, is a collection of stories that answers, fantastically, the question about daily life in Gila River, where Kiik's grandparents, Yoshikane and Peggy, were incarcerated, got married, and had their first child. When Peggy (Margaret in the book) was pregnant, she craved hamburgers, so Kane snuck out of camp to get meat by hiding in the back of a bread truck. Years later, as Kane was dying, Kiik wrote the story, changing hamburgers to whiskey, the bread truck to his grandfather being able to fly. There is a heartbreaking realism to the extremity of daily life, to the profound and impossible ways that time is not only endured but invented. All of the stories in *The Book of Kane and Margaret* feature characters named Yoshikane Araki (Kane) and/or Margaret Morri.

Peggy was born Eiko. When she was young, a teacher told her that she had to choose a new name, and suggested Peggy or Margaret. Before Eiko could answer, her teacher said, "Peggy." After Peggy passed away, in 2022, a white butterfly appeared in the Araki-Kawaguchi's garden. Again and again, almost daily. "It would linger until we'd give it our full attention," said Kiik's mother, Corinne. "Her death during the pandemic broke my heart, and seeing this butterfly helped me to mend."

"In thinking of my grandmother, in conjuring her, I feel her rage," Brynn Saito told me. "Her bitterness. Her hurt. I can also remember her laughter and joy. I wonder, sometimes, if emotions are communal, intergenerational."

In Brynn's poem "Alma, 1942," her grandmother, who was incarcerated in Gila River, seems skeptical of Brynn's curiosity about camp.[69] After sharing a litany of condensed recollections—"To begin they gave us one army blanket / and one army cot, / no doors on the bathroom stalls / and no stoves for heat / only mouthfuls of dust / and the sight of a mountain / in the barbed distance"—Alma addresses Brynn:

> You'll see it for yourself
> when you go there roving
> with your questions for the barracks
> like a hungry ghost.

Is that how our grandparents—bemused, embarrassed, however they love us and *want* us to listen—see us, as hungry ghosts? Insatiable, damned, but a grandmother does

---

69. Brynn Saito, "Alma, 1942," *Palace of Contemplating Departure* (Los Angeles: Red Hen Press, 2013)

not mean it that way, does she? All descendants, then, are hungry ghosts, wandering the world desperate for connection, reciprocation.

Brynn wrote the poem at night, in the dark (the lights were off). It was "as if my tiny, sturdy, white-haired grandmother were standing above me," she said, in an interview.[70] Her grandmother did not talk very much about camp, although Brynn, as she told me, remembers hearing her grandmother "talk bitterly about being *packed in like sardines* on the trains."

Earlier in the poem, Alma asks Brynn a question about how, really why, she plans to research and write about a past that, one could imagine, she herself does not want to revisit:

> So what will you do
> with your curious pen
> and your questions like daggers
> slicing through the ripe heat
> of the merciless summer,
> tearing the grapes from the vine
> till they drop like a satchel
> of dead knuckles on dead earth?

The grandparent, in her skepticism, begins to envision the ruins of her own experience. In asking about her grandchild's return, she is enacting her own. For the grandchild, returning to a place she has never been is to risk trespassing on those who were not able to leave, and to risk keeping them there. What remains, swallowed by ripe heat and dead earth, is not only her grandparent's experience, but her own, because what remains is the source of a silence into which she was born, and that her work, her poetry, is hoping to redeem.

---

70. Karissa Chen, Q&A with poet Brynn Saito, Hyphen, January 27, 2013

"If the silence spoke, what would it say?" Brynn asks, in the interview. ("Maybe it's the most open text. The loudest form of speaking we have," writes Victoria Chang, about silence, in *Dear Memory*. "But silence is a *place* in which to scream!" writes Gwendolyn Brooks in *In the Mecca*.)

What is ironic, both sorrowful and funny, is that by not answering our questions, or answering only slightly—by being a simultaneously accessible and evasive repository of fading experience—grandparents *become the barracks*. The barracks ask questions too, they are curious too.

In the summer of 2019, Brynn and her father, Gregg, visited Gila River, where Alma, then Teranishi, and Mitsuo Saito (Gregg's parents) met and married. She recorded her experience in a series of letters to family—including her grandparents—and friends, which she published in a chapbook, *Dear—*. The final letter is addressed to the reader and includes questions I imagine being asked, in all seriousness, towards an understanding of what daily life is like *here, now*: "Do you believe in the wide open privacy of the desert? Do you believe in the prophecy of stones? Do you feel the distant, silent company of the women in your family—the continuity of the clandestine? Do you memorialize violence; do you ritualize joy?"

She asks these questions again in "Dear Reader," the first poem in *Under a Future Sky*, but with an additional question:

Were you afraid
of what you might say to yourself in the face
of the page's stillness, under the hailstorms
of an arid high desert?

Gila River is the only incarceration site that requires tribal permission to enter. The Gila River Indian Community was occupied from July 1942 to November 1945 in the form of a concentration camp in which 13,348 Japanese immigrants and Japanese Americans were incarcerated, making it, between those dates, the fourth-largest city in Arizona. Phoenix, Tucson, Poston. Gila River was recommended by the Bureau of Indian Affairs, Soil Conservation, and US Forestry, with the intention of using incarcerated labor to develop (colonize) Indigenous land. The tribal council rejected the proposal. The BIA, with whom the WRA shared personnel (Dillon Myer oversaw both. He had the "tendency to collapse the two racial groups," as Ruth Okimoto writes, and wanted the Japanese Americans to "melt or boil away"[71]), spun incarceration as an opportunity for the community to prove their loyalty, but it was a ruse, construction of the camp was already underway. "The history of Japanese American incarceration," writes Hana Maruyama, "starkly reveals the processes through which settler colonialism dispossesses American Indians, destroys the land through resource extraction and promotes white settler property—using racialized incarcerated labor to do it."[72]

From my talk at the Holocaust History Center: "There was an agricultural engineer named Thomas Campbell. He was also the Special Investigator of Native American lands for the Department of the Interior. He was obsessed with the number of what he considered *worthless parcels of real estate*, that were, in the 1930s and 40s, spread throughout the US, much of it being, in Campbell's estimation, on Native reservations. He was also obsessed with the number of reclamation/rehabilitation projects that were under-funded or had

71. Iyko Day, "Japanese Internment and the Mutation of Labor," *Alien Capital* (Durham, NC: Duke University Press, 2016)
72. Hana Maruyama, How Japanese American Incarceration Was Entangled With Indigenous Dispossession, KCET.org, August 18, 2022

been abandoned. Shortly after Pearl Harbor, Campbell had an idea: what if the Japanese in the US—American citizens, Japanese nationals, whoever, it did not matter to Campbell—were rounded up and detained in Army-style camps situated on those *worthless parcels*, so that they could be used as free, captive labor for all of those projects? Campbell noted the number of irrigation and food-production and soil-conservation and road-building projects that could benefit. The Japanese had established themselves as the most industrious and productive agricultural workers in the nation, a fact which should have inspired white farmers and landowners, but enraged them instead. White farmers and landowners wanted the Japanese eliminated. They were among the most fervent advocates for incarceration, petitioning legislators to devise policies to erode the rights of the Japanese. Campbell's idea, meanwhile, accommodated both Japanese industriousness and productivity and white anxiety and rage. He shared his plan with FDR, and then slipped out the back door of history." Thomas Campbell is, as Michi Nishiura Weglyn writes in *Years of Infamy: The Untold Story of America's Concentration Camps*, "a name lost to history despite the considerable impetus and direction he appears to have given the evolving program at the time."

In the end, development and destruction in Gila River were the same. "The WRA sold off what buildings and materials it could, bulldozed the rest, and left mostly unusable rubble in its wake," writes Hana Maruyama. As Iyko Day points out in *Alien Capital: Asian Racialization and the Logic of Settler Colonial Capitalism*, "the outcome was clearly advantageous mostly to white people, who benefited from the access to irrigation systems in the desert, in addition to the dispossessed Japanese property on the West Coast."

There were fifty of us, a small number of whom had been incarcerated, a smaller number at Gila River. We met at a gas station, then followed, in our cars, two men from the tribal council, their white minivan turning up dust. Olive trees looked, in the dust, like smoke. The dust cleared to reveal a white egret on a mound of dirt beside a canal. When we arrived at the base of a saddle-shaped hill, we were handed black plastic bags and told to spread out. Our voices grew louder, somehow closer, more precise. Lisa and I walked up the hill to the water tower foundation, started picking up broken bottles. Spray-painted on the foundation was the couplet:

FUCK THE COPS
HE LOVES ME.

The people below, in the creosote and saguaro, among the concrete foundations and footing blocks, looked like they were carrying ashes, seeking the right place to spread them. The fields of cotton, spare that November, resembled snow, which added an air of refreshment. Agronomists say Arizona cotton is exceptionally white because it never rains in the desert, rain is dirty, but who can look at a field of cotton without seeing generations of bodies ground to dirt?

Did you have anyone in camp? Did you have anyone in Gila River? Did you have anyone in the 442nd? These were the questions most frequently asked. Not once, but all day. The monument at Gila River, for example, which looks like a smile with its teeth knocked out, was built to commemorate the Nisei who died in the war. "Sacrifices were made by these Americans," says the plaque.

During the war, the JACL supported the draft, convinced the Nisei to answer the War Department's call to serve overseas, and condemned, even advocated charging with sedition, those who refused. Although the accomplishments of the 442nd Regimental Combat Team, a segregated, all-Nisei unit, were real and voluminous—they were awarded several Distinguished Unit Citations, hundreds of Silver Stars and Distinguished Service Crosses, thousands of Bronze Stars and Purple Hearts—so was their exploitation. Eight hundred Nisei were killed or went missing.

What about the sacrifices made by the Japanese Americans who did not die in the war, who served in the opacity of their barracks, behind bars, in a state of condemnation? Approximately 300 Nisei resisted the draft or refused to accept it unless their rights as citizens were restored.[73] It was clear, to them, that loyalty, however it might be proven, did not ensure equality, a fact underscored by the 442nd being a segregated unit. The JACL's condemnation formed an attitude that had tremendous influence, especially on how the community viewed itself—how it absorbed, talked about, and embodied loyalty and allegiance, how it understood itself as American, and how it understood it had to become, and keep becoming, American.

When I attended the Minidoka Pilgrimage in 2023, the feature that seemed to draw out the most outward displays of emotion was the restored Honor Roll. The three-panel signboard, standing, proudly, at the entrance to camp, lists nearly 1,000 Japanese Americans in Minidoka who served in the war. People touched the names, cried, held each other. Because it was at the entrance, people had to confront it, ask it questions. Which it answered, explicitly. Beneath the wings of the bald eagle mounted at the top of the signboard were two bitterly ironic quotes, both chosen by the Japanese Americans: one from Secretary of War Henry Stimson: "It is the inherent right of every faithful

---

73. The largest concentrations of resisters were in Poston and in Heart Mountain, where they were organized by the Fair Play Committee. Resisters were sent to federal prison—Leavenworth (Kansas), McNeil Island (Washington), Tucson (Arizona).

citizen, regardless of ancestry, to bear arms in the nation's battle"; the other from FDR: "Americanism is a matter of the mind and heart; Americanism is not, and never was, a matter of race or ancestry."

Later that day, in a healing circle—ten of us in a room sharing our thoughts and feelings about the pilgrimage— one of the survivors talked about people he knew who were in the 442nd, how they just wanted to protect each other, keep each other from dying. How they just wanted to go the fuck home. He was a child in camp, but if he had been old enough, he said, he would not have gone to war. And yet, listening to his friends, he understood it was not a choice, there were no sides. They hated it, they hated fight- ing, it was not as simple as saying there were some who fought to prove their loyalty and some who refused because they did not believe they needed to prove anything, or that there were some who were tricked into fighting to prove their loyalty to an uncaring country and those who were not tricked, who saw, clearly and through, the country's complete lack of care. Everyone, even the children who were born hours before the camps were closed, was at war.

Eighty Nisei men were incarcerated in the Leupp Isolation Center on Navajo Nation, Arizona. They were originally incarcerated with their families in camp, then, for resisting their mistreatment, were labeled "troublemakers" and sent to a Navajo boarding school. Executive Orders 9066 and 9102 were used "to claim exceptional spatial jurisdictions on the Navajo Indian Reservation," and permitted the WRA to "intentionally bypass and disregard the sovereign power of the Navajo Tribal Council."[74] Some of the Nisei were

---

74. Lynne Horiuchi, Spatial Jurisdictions, Historical Topographies, and Sovereignty at the Leupp Isolation Center, *Amerasia Journal*, 42:1, 2016

transported "on the back of a flat-bed truck in a coffin-like box, in which, wedged together in a five-by-six-foot space with only a small hole in back for air, they nearly suffocated."[75] Eighty Nisei, but 150 military police, four guard towers, a cyclone fence with barbed wire. The Nisei were barred from interacting with the Navajo. The Navajo were instructed not to speak with the Nisei. But the trading post was next door. The Navajo gave the Nisei food, the Nisei learned Yá'át'ééh and said it back through the fence.

The boarding school opened in 1909, closed in 1942. There were five hundred children. Parents who did not send their children were jailed. The trading post did not close until 1980. There is, on the present-day map, an empty square labeled simply: "Depression."

Minutes after Pearl Harbor, the staff of the Japanese consulate in Honolulu was arrested. They were detained in the consulate for ten days while the State Department searched for a remote location—unpopulated, yet with enough infrastructure for it to be turned, quickly and surreptitiously, into a prison. Lake Tahoe, Tucson, Patagonia, the Triangle T Ranch in Dragoon, an unincorporated community of about forty people. The land occupied by the Triangle T had been a winter camp for the Chiricahua Apaches. For almost fifty years, between the signing of the Treaty of Guadalupe Hidalgo in 1848, and their being exiled to Fort Sill, the Chiricahua Apaches were removed and relocated innumerable times throughout the Southwest and as far east as Florida.

The Japanese—including Nagao Kita, the Consul General, and his family—were taken to San Diego aboard the USS President Hayes, by train to Tucson, then into a desert where the rocks resembled people. All signage on the roads

75. Harry Ueno, *Manzanar Martyr* (Fullerton, CA: California State University, Fullerton, Oral History Program, 1986)

was removed, as were all the stamps on the luggage. The Triangle T knew that a group of people were coming but they did not know who or where they were from.

The ranch was empty, except for two white men sitting at the bar. Last night, they said, was hoppin', which was difficult to imagine in a town of so few people. The population of Dragoon has not changed much since the Japanese. There is a post office, a church, an art gallery in someone's yard, and, near the cemetery, a women's club and a thrift store. Dirt roads lead from the Triangle T to the Amerind Museum of Indigenous culture and crafts.

One of the men, in cowboy hat and handlebar mustache, introduced himself as the owner of the ranch. "This is where the Japanese were roaming around," he said. We were on the front porch, looking out on a landscape where one could imagine hot springs flowing, but there was no water. "See that metal post up there?" He pointed to a rock resembling a person. "That's where one of the guard towers was."

The prison was staffed by Border Patrol. Kita and his family stayed in a casita, while everyone else—secretaries and officials, servants, the consulate's gardeners, all of their children—was crammed into horse stalls. "A lot of tourists come here to take pictures of it," the owner said, of the horse stalls. "Because of the movie."

"What movie?" I asked.

"*3:10 to Yuma,*" he said.

When I told him I hadn't seen it, he gave me a look like, *Then why are you here?*

I peered through the slats of the horse stall. Two wooden chairs, covered in dust, faced each other, as if two ghosts were having a conversation. Which ghosts? You cannot, in such landscapes, be sure.

After my talk, as people were leaving the Holocaust History Center, a man came up to me, pointed at the ceiling, and said, "The young girl with the enormous bow is my cousin." Hanging from the rafters were photographs of people who had been murdered in the Holocaust, including a young girl with an enormous bow. "Her name is Etta," the man said. "She was murdered before I was born."

Joel. He was born in the US near the end of the war. He told me that when he was young he did not think the Holocaust had anything to do with his family. When he was in his twenties, his grandfather, who immigrated to the US from Lithuania, revealed to him that many people in their family had died in the Holocaust. "A large family was lost," he said. Joel, inspired to find traces of the large family, traveled to Europe. He met one of his relatives, Abramson. During the war, Abramson was sent to Dachau. His wife and two children—Etta and Yossi (also in the rafters)—were sent to a death camp, Joel could not remember which one. Abramson survived. After Dachau—liberated by Japanese Americans, the 522nd Field Artillery Battalion, which was originally part of the 442nd—Abramson met a woman in Munich, who offered to give him food from her family's garden. They married and had a child, a daughter. Abramson named her Itta. He did not tell Itta or his wife where the name came from. It was not until he died that Itta learned about Etta. Itta was the one who gave Joel the photograph. He donated it to the museum. It is difficult to resist projecting emotions onto the face of someone who has died, but that is the mind-boggling condition of a photograph, and the identity it holds back: it was not a photograph of a young girl who had been murdered. Etta was, in the photograph, alive. She looked, despite her young age, world-weary. Her bow was as large as her face and so lustrous it seemed you could, if you reached into the rafters, bring it down, and Etta with it, into the room.

I dedicated my talk to my great-aunt Joy. She was four when her family was sent to Santa Anita. They were living in Alhambra; Joy's father, Frank Shigeo Mastumoto, owned a produce business, which he had to give up. Frank's friends, a German American family (the Lauvachs), took care of their belongings while they were gone.

They moved into a horse stall. Joy remembered her mother, Hama Matsumoto, constantly sneezing. Then they were on a train. They did not know where they were going, if it would be better or worse. When I asked Joy what she remembered about Poston, the first thing she said was, "dust."

The Colorado River Indian Reservation was occupied by the WRA from June 1942 to November 1945 in the form of a concentration camp in which 17,814 Japanese immigrants and Japanese Americans were incarcerated, making it, between those dates, the third-largest city in Arizona. Phoenix, Tucson. As in Gila River, the tribal council rejected the proposal.

It was even more difficult after the war, Joy told me. They were welcomed back to California by anti-Japanese signs. Houses were shot at. She and her family lived for one year in a hostel in Boyle Heights. Their room fit two beds, nothing more. "That's the reason you did not grow very tall," Joy's mother told her. They moved to Pacoima, then Pasadena, then Beverly Hills, where they lived with a white family. In exchange, Frank did their gardening, Hama their housecleaning. Joy remembers being fed the family's scraps. She remembers the fat from the white family's meat.

Joy did not talk with her children about camp. No one in the family talked about it, including Joy's uncle, Koya Kurihara, who was in the 442nd. "It was off-limits," Dean Yamashita, Joy's son, told me. What little he knew he heard from his neighbor, Masao Shono, from Terminal

Island. Mas was always talking about Japanese American history—with Dean's father in the garage, with Dean in the yard. He was a poet, taught Dean haiku. Dean gave a presentation in high school. He covered general facts: the number of incarcerees, where they were from, how long it lasted. He described the barracks, the barbed wire, the guard towers. "From what I remember, the majority of the class had no idea this happened," he told me.

When he was in his thirties, he went with his mother to Poston. His first time there, her first time back. "It was calm, quiet, serene," he told me. "I stuck close to my mother and just listened."

When Joy was young, she had a recurring dream about airplanes flying overhead. "The noise," she said. When Dean was in his late twenties, he dreamed about guard towers. "Visions," he said. Six times over the decade: guard towers, empty. "I never saw a face."

YOU MAY NOT BE ON MY TIME YET

WHEN CATHLIN GOULDING WAS IN HER TWENTIES, SHE saw, at a film festival in San Jose, Dave Tatsuno's 8mm home movies from Topaz. Out of approximately seventy-five shots and scenes—of barracks, the mess hall, pigs in a pen, a dust storm, women, children, snow, mountains, sunrises, sunsets—Goulding remembered one scene in particular: a woman in a bright red sweater "ice-skating around a tiny rink in the desert."[76]

The image, without sound, has the quality of a dream recollected. The woman is the only person on the ice. ("No one had skates," Tatsuno says, in voiceover. "This young lady is the only one." "Did she bring them with her?" Goulding wondered. "Did she order them from one of those Sears catalogs?") She skates slowly, thoughtfully, as if she too is trying to remember a dream. Tatsuno films her from above and far away—is he on the roof of a barrack?—then close up, even closer, her skates. She must have been skating a long time for Tatsuno to capture so many

---

76. Cathlin Goulding, This Must Be The Place: Designing Places of Exception as Places of Learning, Teachers College, Columbia University, May 17, 2017

perspectives. Or, time stops, or she becomes time. "She spins around in circles, crinkling her face in laughter."[77]

"Sometimes the woman in the red sweater appeared in my dreams," Goulding writes. "When I woke up from these dreams, there was always an initial, startled moment of confusion: Was the woman a part of my memories? Or the memories of others?"[78]

"What happens in the dreams?" I asked her.

"A lot of times it will be a mesh of dreams about my mother and these bridges that she's on one side of and I'm on the other side of," Goulding told me. "It's always about a figure that's out of reach."

"Where is the ice skater?"

"It's different flashes. She's one flash, and my mother is another."

"I was back on the strawberry farm," said Jordan Adams, "but it was part of the camp. We were working in the fields but surrounded by fences and my mother was wearing the long-sleeve arm coverings that my great-grandmother used to wear."

"I'm watching my grandmother interacting with the army nurse who *re-named* her because her Japanese name would *cause trouble*," said Chelsey Oda. "I want to interject but I'm like a ghostly observer who nobody can see or hear."

"My nightmares frequently present a lack of agency and control," said Sara Onitsuka. "I am being chased; I am trapped. I am forced to pretend that I am going along with the plans of my captors in order to escape."

---

77. Cathlin Goulding, This Must Be The Place, op. cit.
78. Ibid.

"No escape," said Patricia Saito Hecht. "Not able to see, hear, touch, smell, be with my family and friends. Alone. A terrifying feeling, utterly hopeless, trapped."

"I am outside," said Brett Esaki. "The overall context is prison, but there are moments when beauty is possible. I do not see any prison bars, barbed wire, or guards, but the aching feeling is present."

"I was in a dusty desert prison camp," said Mas Moriya, "but updated with lockers for personal items. I had a key, or found a key, that went to a locker, and found a gun in that locker. I made sure to hide the gun for later in case something happened. I remember feeling that this was a decision I didn't want to make but had to, to save myself."

"I was running around the camp trying to find a gap in the barbed wire fence," said Alexis Ajioka, "not to go anywhere (it is in the middle of the desert after all) but just to be outside of the walls."

"A frequent motif in my dreams is being forced to use a filthy public bathroom with no privacy," said Katherine Terumi Laubscher. "The walls of the stalls are short or non-existent, there are no doors, and there are lots of other people. The toilets and the floors are dirty, but I know I have no choice.

"As a child, maybe elementary school age, I had a recurring dream that I was walking around in a cypress swamp," said Lauren Sumida. "The trees were growing out of the water with wide trunks and root systems jutting out. It was always very serene and peaceful, even though I was alone in the swamp just walking around. I don't think I'd ever seen any cypress swamps before in real life, but then when we were on the bus in Arkansas going from

Little Rock to McGehee, we drove by pockets of forest swamps that looked right out of that childhood dream, or at least enough that I was immediately reminded of the dreamscape."

"I remember a desert landscape," said Alyssa Watanabe Kapaona. "Totally barren, just sand, rocks, wind. Brown, rocky mountains. I don't remember any green plants. I can't really see due to the sand and the wind and I can't breathe due to inhaling sand or dust when I try to breathe."

"Sometimes I'll see sand for miles surrounded by mountains and I feel and see the sun," said Natalia Arai. "So bright and hot. There's no one there. There's no shelter or shade. Other times I feel the sand in my throat and I wake up coughing. Other times I feel it in my eyes and it burns. Other times I look at my hands and they're painfully dry. Chapped and bleeding."

"I've had dreams about the dust and how endless the sky looks," said Emily Merolli, "broken only by a reconstructed guard tower, the reclaimed water tower, and a reconstructed barrack. The air warm and dry, constantly moving in unpredictable swirls, kicking dust over the tall balsamroot, blowing them clean again. These are the characteristics of incarceration that haunted my obasan, but they're oddly comforting to me. I feel settled, connected, and purposeful. There's never anyone else physically present, but I'm definitely not alone."

"I woke with the realization that camp ended," said Brynn Saito, "and that they had to leave and go back into the world, their lives. That time, I woke crying."

"I have never seen my father weep," said Willitte Hisami Ishii Herman. "I have an early image I have grown up with that perhaps was a dream, of seeing my father sitting in a straight-backed chair, his arms rigid, palms gripping his knees, an anguished grimace on his face. Whether this is memory or dream that has long shimmered behind my eyes, I do not know."

"I often visit with those I know as my dead in dreams," said Emily Mitamura. "They give me advice and often closure. They show me how to be kind to myself and when something is over."

"Once, I scooped my grandma Chiz up in my arms to shield her from someone/something violent," Mitamura continued. "She took me aside after that and said, *We have to take care of ourselves, we're full of ghosts.* She said it and it felt like a confidence."

"I was sitting on the living room floor of my childhood home with my dad," said Diana Emiko Tsuchida, "and from what I can recall of the atmosphere, it was a family party or some type of lively gathering. A lot of people were in the room, and as my dad and I were talking to each other, I noticed that his dad, my grandfather, was there, too, and motioned for us to sit on the floor with him. He held out his hands to show us an old clock. *You may not be on my time yet*, he said, *but you will be.*

STRAWBERRY FIELDS

"IN 1942, MY GRANDFATHER BURNED THE FAMILY'S POS-sessions in the strawberry fields behind the house," a young woman says, in voiceover. "He thought if he burned them, no one could take their things after they were gone." A match is lit and raised to a piece of gray cloth in the dark. The cloth goes up in flames. "The next morning," the woman continues, "the government sent my mother's family to the internment camps." A girl is playing the piano. When she turns the page of her piano book, a photograph falls out: a man in front of tarpaper barracks. The woman speaking is Irene Kawai (Suzy Nakamura; family in Minidoka), sansei, sixteen. The girl playing the piano is her younger sister, Terri (Heather Yoshimura). The man in the photograph is their grandfather. The barracks behind him are Poston.

These are the opening scenes of Rea Tajiri's *Strawberry Fields* (1997), a film, written with the Japanese Canadian novelist Kerri Sakamoto. In them, the past is extinguished in a desperate, self-protective act, and in that instant, the primary condition of the Kawai family becomes one of loss.

The strawberry fields were the realization of a dream that carried many Issei from Japan to the United States, working against Alien Land Laws, on white-owned/occupied land, through the battery of prisons and detention centers and camps, in which the dream was stretched, tested ("when the strawberry juice   ran down your chin / and we disappeared...did you think you'd ever see us again?"[79]), back to the strawberry fields they left, that were no longer there ("the red juice flows between your teeth / with the memory of strawberries"[80]).

Strawberry Fields was the first film I saw, of any kind, with an entirely Japanese American cast. That this occurred around the subject of incarceration suggested, to me, what it meant when Japanese Americans gathered, or were gathered, together: the barbed wire was coming out again. But there is no barbed wire in *Strawberry Fields*. The film, even though it goes there, is not about camp, but about what it became. At some point in the telling of the story, barbed wire, so fully absorbed into the psyche, became redundant. Karen Ishizuka, sansei, refers to it as "barbed wire of the mind." Filmmaker Daryn Wakasa, yonsei, refers to it as barbed wire in the veins.

   Strawberry Fields was also the first film I saw about incarceration that centered the experience and perspective of the descendant, which brought with it the suggestion that the conditions and repercussions of camp were now embodied by those who were not there. And because it centered this experience and perspective, it eliminated the need for the most cliché, and the most gratuitous, of characters: the white love interest and/or savior. Many of the films I had seen until then, *Come See the Paradise*, *Snow Falling on Cedars*, *The Magic of Ordinary Days*, managed,

79. Anne Yukie Watanabe, "instructions to, 1942," *The Gate of Memory: Poems by Descendants of Nikkei Wartime Incarceration* (Chicago: Haymarket Books, 2025)
80. David Mura, Issei Strawberry, *The Colors of Desire* (New York: Anchor Books, 1995)

against the objection of reality, to center one or the other, usually both, in the form of the same earnest yet hopeless white person. "Films like these," write Elena Tajima Creef in *Imaging Japanese America*, "suggest that Japanese American history has little relevance for white spectators unless the latter can literally see themselves as central players in the script." They "render white liberal American heroes the true subject of wartime oppression and suffering."

Strawberry Fields takes place in 1971. Title II of the Internal Security Act of 1950, aka the Emergency Detention Act, aka the *concentration camp law*—granting the government authority to detain, under the guise of national security, any individual suspected of having committed or even *intending* to commit an act of espionage or sabotage—was repealed. American crimes in Southeast Asia, outlined by the Pentagon Papers, released in 1971, were in their sixteenth year. Student uprisings led to the creation of the first Asian American Studies programs, at San Francisco State, UC Berkeley, and UCLA, where the first issue of *Amerasia Journal* and the first Asian American Studies textbook, *Roots: An Asian American Reader*, were published. "These are critical times for Asian Americans," Franklin Odo wrote, in the preface to *Roots*, "and it is imperative that their voices be heard in all their anger, anguish, resolve and inspiration."

Irene Kawai is angry. She lights matches compulsively, flicks them at strangers. Jumps out the window of her high school classroom, runs away. Fights with her mother (Marilyn Tokuda; family in Minidoka), who is closed off, hiding something. When Irene sees the photograph of her grandfather, she is overwhelmed with questions. Where is he? What is he doing? It is the beginning of her suspicion that her anger might be the embodiment of a question, and that an answer might be found wherever it is her grandfather is standing.

She goes to a party. A woman is playing "We Are the Children" on guitar. "We are the children of the migrant workers, we are the offspring of the concentration camps."[81] Irene stands, uncomfortably, in the hallway and stares at a poster on the wall: a dark sea of monochromatic military barracks beneath a white sky on which is emblazoned:

IT HAS HAPPENED HERE.
IT COULD HAPPEN AGAIN — TO YOU!

A man (Chris Tashima; family in Gila River and Poston) presses a medallion-size drug into Irene's hand. "It's medicinal," he says. Irene takes it and locks herself in the bathroom. She smears toothpaste all over the mirror, rubs her face in the toothpaste. She finds a gun under the sink and aims it at her reflection. The sound of glass shattering, but the mirror is intact, there is no gun. Someone knocks on the door. Terri—who has, by this point in the film, died—appears. "You're dead!" Irene says. "*You're* dead!" Terri taunts back. The knocking gets louder. Irene's friends break into the bathroom, drag her out. "Come out now you little snatch!" she screams, fighting off her friends. "Come out now you snatch!"

Who is she screaming at? Everyone, including her dead sister, seems to know more than she does—about the past, about what is plaguing her, that what is plaguing her is the past. How do they know so much? Or, rather, how does Irene know so little? "And what is the role of *historical withholding* in the transmission of trauma?" asks Marianne Hirsch, in *The Generation of Postmemory*.

---

81. Chris Iijima, Nobuko Miyamoto, Charlie Chin, "We Are the Children," *A Grain of Sand: Music for the Struggle by Asians in America* (Paredon Records, 1973)

Irene travels with her friend Aura (Reiko Mathieu, Tajiri's cousin) from Chicago to Poston. Aura suggests they visit a woman named Takayo (Takayo Fischer; incarcerated in Rohwer) who was incarcerated in Poston.

"She's still there," Aura says. "She could help."

When they arrive, Takayo is kneeling in the garden. She looks up at the women with the expression of someone who has been hiding a long time and has been caught, and as if the sudden appearance of these Asian women startles her into a reminder that she has never left her prison.

She goes inside, changes clothes, puts on makeup. Dresses up for history, as if for a reunion. She regales Irene and Aura with stories from camp, sings "Shina No Yoru." "My daddy sang that," Irene says. "It was kind of a camp song," Takayo says. She pulls a record out of its sleeve, puts it on—"Shina No Yoru," performed by the Club Nisei Orchestra, Sparky Iwamoto singing. "Something he didn't burn," she says, referring to Irene's grandfather. How does she know that? The way she says it suggests that they were close, enough for her to know that he burned the family's possessions. Is Takayo the one who took the photograph that fell out of the piano book? Was she waiting for someone, maybe even Irene, to appear? With that nearly subliminal revelation, Takayo leaves the room. Irene takes the record off the player, and breaks it over her knee.

Because this is no longer about history.

In *Come See the Paradise* (dir. Allan Parker, 1990), the Kawamura family is given six days to evacuate. "What are we going to do with these old records?" they say. "They're all Japanese, no one's going to buy them." "Break them," Lily, the oldest sibling (Tamlyn Tomita; family in Manzanar and Heart Mountain), says. They smash the records on the floor. One remains on the record player: a Japanese man singing. Lily lifts it off the player and breaks it.

In *Farewell to Manzanar* (the book), Jeanne Wakatsuki Houston's mother is forced to sell the family's china, worth at least $200. The secondhand dealers are "like wolves." One of them offers $15. Mama, enraged, smashes a plate at his feet. The wolf howls, "Those are valuable!" It is only after he is deprived of what he intended to steal that he admits to the plates' value. Mama smashes another plate, then another, until the wolf "scuttles," like a cockroach, out the door. The floor becomes a ruin of "blue and white fragments." In the film version (dir. John Korty, 1976), when Mama (Nobu McCarthy) breaks the dishes at the man's feet, the look on her face is a blazing combination of anger, devastation, and hopelessness.

I asked Tajiri if her family burned or buried or gave away or lost any of their possessions prior to removal. "My father's mother locked their Japanese heirlooms in a closet, then they rented out their house," she said.

Then the house disappeared.

"The neighborhood was condemned by the US government," Tajiri said, "then seized under eminent domain. As I understood it, all the houses were sold and the government paid to have each one moved."

"For a long time the government denied that the house ever existed," said Roberto Ryukichi Santiago, Tajiri's cousin. "Now that street is part of the naval base in San Diego."

"The story sometimes went that it was literally stolen off its foundations," said Vince Schleitwiler, scholar, writer, and Tajiri's nephew. "The circulation of the story might be more telling than whatever really happened. I've tried to write in several different places about the trope, in fictional and nonfictional stories about incarceration, about the burning (or burial) of family heirlooms, Japanese-language materials, and the like, which I think is about a desire to preserve some aspect of a familial or communal past in a space beyond representation. What's burned or buried, like the bodies of loved ones who have died, is not so much gone as secreted in an inaccessible realm that is beyond the reach of those who would do you harm, or misconstrue or appropriate what is yours. And I tend to be critical of uses of this trope that imply that the accounts themselves, subsequent and usually by children or grandchildren, can reclaim this lost inheritance by returning it to the realm of representation (the story itself as the recovery of whatever was lost). In particular, in certain Japanese American writing the trope gets turned from immolation to conflagration—the burning of the treasured objects becomes linked to fire as a destructive but liberating force in an unjust order."

It is not until a fragment is found that it becomes, paradoxically, missing. The breaking of records, of plates, the burning of possessions in the strawberry fields: shattering the past, removing each fragment from its context. When the descendant arrives, the past appears, if at all, as a mass of indistinguishable fragments, enclosing within it a star chart of negative space that the descendant feels compelled to decode and complete.

"I just had this fragment, this picture that's always been in my mind," Tajiri says, in her documentary *History and Memory* (1991). "My mother, she's standing at a faucet, and it's really hot outside, and she's filling this canteen, and the water is really cold and it feels really good, and outside the sun is just so hot, it's just beating down, and there's this dust that gets in everywhere, and they're always sweeping the floors." A woman in a blue sweater holds a canteen up to a stream of water, then holds her hands up to the water to wash her face. The woman—the image—appears several times throughout the film, sometimes from behind, sometimes just her face, her hands. "For years I've been living with this picture without the story, feeling a lot of pain, not knowing how they fit together."

Later in the film, Tajiri remembers her way back into the realization that the image was from a story that she overheard her mother telling her sister. It was the only time she heard her mother speaking openly about camp. Even then, it revolved around a single, however shimmering, impression.

Ten of Tajiri's family members, including her mother, Rose, were incarcerated in Santa Anita, Salinas, and Poston. "Right before I was going to make *History and Memory*, I started being very direct," Tajiri told me. "My mother acted very strange as though she had amnesia. I started to do research in the National Archives and I found her camp records. I went to the hotel room that night and called her. I felt like I was interrogating her—I could not believe how strange her voice got—and that she was denying she was in camp."

After finishing *History and Memory*, Tajiri played it for her mother. She put it on the TV and left the room. When Tajiri came back, the screen was black, and her mother, sitting in front of it, was nodding soundlessly to herself.

On the screen: black-and-white photographs of Poston being built (razed desert, wooden frames transforming into barracks looking, despite the summer heat, cold; built by Del Webb, who took what he learned from the concentration camp and applied it to building a dystopian suburban development for retirees, Sun City) yield to footage of Poston, forty years later: concrete slabs and dilapidated buildings, waterlogged and punched-in, surrounded by tall weeds and puddles of rain.[82]

---

82. When Irene Kawai arrives in Poston, there are no buildings, no weeds, just flat, uninterrupted desert.

When I asked Elizabeth Ito, animator and the creator of *City of Ghosts*, what she imagined of Gila River, where her grandfather, Ted Ito, a cartoonist, was incarcerated, she said, "I imagine the sound of wind."

When I asked Sean Miura, writer and producer/curator of Little Tokyo's Tuesday Night Cafe, where he goes to be with his ancestors, he said, "I am with them when there is wind."

In the documentary *And Then They Came For Us* (2017, dirs. Abby Ginzberg and Ken Schneider), Satsuki Ina is standing in the ruins of Topaz talking about her parents, her mother, the wind. "My mother wrote in her diary about this wind," she says. "It was here that they really felt the peak of their despair. When I read her diary, it's one thing," she continues, "but when I'm here, I actually want to feel this wind. It's what they had, you know."

"I went to Idaho because I wanted to walk the same spaces, feel the same sun, hear the same wind," the actor Suzy Nakamura told me. She visited Minidoka for the first time twenty years after visiting Poston as Irene Kawai. She was not, as she told me, very much like her character. Irene's parents are ghosts, detached from their experience. Suzy's parents talked openly about camp. Her father, incarcerated in Tule Lake, was "angry and bitter until the day he died." Her mother, incarcerated in Minidoka—she died the year *Strawberry Fields* began filming—spoke more nostalgically, recalling "idyllic memories, like the first time she rode a train, the first time she left Washington, and the first time she had a job (picking potatoes). She talked about sitting with her friends in the mess hall and cutting school to go ice skating." And yet, as Suzy told me, "she made sure my understanding included the context of wartime paranoia and hysteria."

Suzy shared some of her mother's memories with Takayo Fischer. "We sat on the bed (on set) and started talking about the script and incarceration," Suzy told me. "She said she was having trouble understanding how anyone could remember camp with nostalgia. She couldn't believe a human being would recall the camp experience without bitterness, and I realized that my mom's perspective might be rare."

Suzy attended the Minidoka Pilgrimage in 2017. She walked for miles in the summer heat. The root cellar, a cavernous tunnel, overgrown and harboring wildlife, was still there. The baseball field and small scoreboard, up against farmland, water wheels ticking like cicadas, were still there. The swimming hole, drained, dry, creosote concealing shards of cups and plates, was still there. One of the barracks, which had been used, in the years since, to house migrant farmworkers, was still there. (Carved into one of the walls: "Carlos That me.")

"I was able to write a small note to my mom and her family and leave it there," Nakamura said. "Now that they're gone, it's like I want to be sad and angry for them by proxy."[83]

"You probably remember a scene," the poet Steve Fujimura told me, "in which Suzy Nakamura's character meets the more seasoned activist couple and they are all watching moving images of JAs in camp projected on a makeshift screen. That was the first time I ever saw moving images of Japanese Americans in camp, and I was shocked and mesmerized by them. Something abstract and unclear in my mind had become suddenly and irreversibly real or palpable, and it involved me intimately. It was uncanny. I try to describe it as (like) the process of interpellation (in Althusser's sense) by which encountering and internalizing media (moving images) makes one a *subject* in a story or culture, attaches that person to an ideology, forms an

83. Suzy Nakamura, in an email, March 13, 2021

identity. As if I were to say, I became Japanese American when I saw those moving images."

Time travel: a confrontation with one's origins, one's place in the world. In Daryn Wakasa's film *Seppuku* (2016), a woman commits ritual suicide in the ruins of Manzanar. Mari Yoshimori (Akemi Look) is an Olympic athlete. Despite having suffered a career-ending injury, she refuses to stop training. Alone one night on a flood-lit track, she injures herself again, and is plunged, through her injury, into Manzanar.

The climax takes place at night. The moment is concentrated on Mari's face, her expression between agony and ecstasy. It is not exactly Manzanar that has forced this grisly self-revelation, but the world beyond, the world that seems to have fallen away, that has become the most acute and inescapable revelation of the past, and one that Mari must return to.

"This is reality now, it's not a secret," says June Kuramoto, in Tadashi Nakamura's *Pilgrimage* (2006), a film that narrates the genesis of the Manzanar pilgrimage, and the awakening, within the sansei community especially, of a consciousness about what happened. "And so we have the burden of what do we do with this now."

Is pilgrimage a form of time travel? "No, time travel isn't exactly what it is," writes Kiku Hughes, in *Displacement*. "I'm taken to a different *place* too. Besides, time travel makes it sound like I have a choice in the matter."

"What the camp pilgrimage enacts is not the memorialization but the mobilization of the past, a rite of movement," writes Vince Schleitwiler in "Apparitions of the Non-Alien: Manzanar."

Wakasa had a vision once that he was being led by a deer through a network of cavernous tunnels beneath enormous, moss-covered ruins. Every morning while filming *Seppuku*, he went for a walk around Manzanar. On the final day, as the sun was rising, he heard the sounds of a baseball game, children laughing. Then Manzanar "came alive," he told me. It was a "joyous noise," camp rematerializing around him.

"Then, as if rising from the ground around us on the valley floor, I began to hear the first whispers, nearly inaudible, from all those thousands who once had lived out here," writes Jeanne Wakatsuki Houston, in *Farewell to Manzanar*, "a wide, windy sound of the ghost of that life."

When a descendant returns to the ruins, whether driven, dragged, plunged, forced, or of their own volition, they discover that *they too* are a fragment, a missing piece.

The final scenes of *Strawberry Fields* take place in Poston.[84] Irene is joined by her dead sister Terri. They lie on the ground, hold hands and close their eyes. The scene cuts to Irene pushing a homemade bomb—wooden box, dynamite, wires—across the ground. It starts ticking. Terri sits on it. "I want to stay," she says. Irene tries to pull her off. She does not want her sister to die again. Aura appears, pulls Irene away from the bomb. It detonates, leaving a streak of flame, then a shallow hole in the ground.

"Where is she?" Irene asks.

"There's nobody here but you," Aura says.

---

84. The scenes were filmed in Palmdale, CA.

STARS ABOVE THE RUINS

Have you visited the site or sites where your family members were incarcerated? If so, what was your experience there? What did you see, hear, discover? What of that visit do you remember?

"Haru said she never noticed how beautiful the mountains were," said Reiko Fujii (Manzanar).

"I was amazed by the sight of so many mountains," said Amy Lee-Tai (Topaz). "The mountains that my grandparents[85] had sketched and painted and made woodblock prints of; the mountains they must've longed to walk toward, to climb up and down, toward freedom."

"The sky was as big as I had always imagined," said Elán Rie (Poston).

"A brilliant, deep blue with white clouds billowing over the mountains," said Emily Nakashima (Manzanar).

"Manzanar is absolutely breathtaking in the summer, with the looming mountains and wide desert plains," said Alexis Ajioka (Manzanar), "but it was also hot and oppressive."

---

85. Artists George Matsusaburo Hibi and Hisako Shimizu Hibi

"It hurt to think of them living in the weight of that heat," said Emily Mitamura (Poston).

"The wind was so strong that the power went out in the nearest town," said Esther Matsuda (Manzanar). "We tried to walk in the wind and had to lean into the wind in order to avoid being blown back."

"The distinct smell of horse droppings, the whirling winds from the nearby San Gabriel Mountains, causing hay to cover our shoes or get in our faces," said Kathy Kojimoto (Santa Anita). "It was an unimaginable smell that made us nauseated and angry."

"The feel of hot wind, the sweet smell of wild grasses, the clicking sounds of insects, erased the distance of time." said Emily Merolli (Amache).

"The dust was unbearable," said Kiyoko Merolli (Amache). "It coated my throat as I talked, sending me into a coughing fit."

"I got sand in my eye and it wouldn't stop tearing up and turning red," said Miko Charbonneau (Manzanar). "My grandmother was obsessed with keeping things clean and I wondered if this was why."

"It was an incredibly difficult experience, seeing where my grandmother's barrack was and the bathrooms," Alexis Ajioka continued. "The latter made me afraid for my pre-teen grandmother who would have been cold, alone and exposed. The former made me angry and full of grief. The US was so ready to tear away anything that reminded them of their transgression, that her childhood home, even in a depressing barrack form, no longer exists."

"I remember one woman standing in the space where her barrack would had been," said Kathryn Nishibayashi (Manzanar; family in Heart Mountain and Jerome), "and saying, *That's where the bathroom was*, even though no building was there."

"I remember the lack of anything that would point to human existence," said Jill Kunishima (Rohwer; family also in Crystal City and Minidoka), "just a handful of gravestones, which seems fitting—this was not a place for the living."

"I remember small stone ruins near the road," Emily Nakashima continued. "They smelled like thousands of passing motorists had peed on them over the years."

"The swamp had been *drained* and most of the trees were cut down," said Julie Kanazawa (Rohwer).

"It was barren and ungodly hot, not a tree in the ground, no shade," said Michael Kawana (Poston).

"Everything was so drab and unwelcoming," Kiyoko Merolli continued.

"I felt a strong sense of sadness because the place was much harsher than I had imagined," said Aisuke Kondo (Topaz).

"My memory of it was that it was bleak, spacious, windy," said Elizabeth Ito (Manzanar). My mental image is like that giant salt flat where they have Burning Man, but I don't think it was quite that bad. The colors are similar though, a lot of white, and dust, and shrubs."

"We were all surprised that the land seemed lush and green, not like the historic photos of the dry desert," said Michelle Kumata (Minidoka)

"We were all so surprised to see the *camp* bursting with beautiful wildflowers," said Karen Kiyo Lowhurst (Heart Mountain).

"We saw many of the gardens that people built," said Koji Lau-Ozawa (Gila River), "the footprints of buildings, the scars of construction, the flora and fauna of the desert, including Gila monsters, coyotes, a mountain lion, javelina, rattlesnakes, wild horses, saguaro cactus (Ha:shan), mesquite (Kui), creosote (Shegoi), cholla (Hannam), ironwood (Ho'ithkam), ocotillo (Melhog)."[86]

"I remember looking at the fields and being confused how this used to be a camp when it's now just a bunch of fields growing crops," said Micah Tasaka (Poston).

"We were pretty horrified to discover that the land had been turned into an alfalfa farm," Elán Rie continued.

"The farmer who owned the property was very nice and accommodating," said Carol Mayeda (Jerome), "and he showed us the only remnant from the camp: a cement slab."

"The owner of the land at the memorial was present and, while he was welcoming to all, I felt uncomfortable—like I was trespassing on someone else's property," Julie Kanazawa continued.

"There was no interpretive center," said Carl Takei (Manzanar; family also in Amache, Fort Bliss, Fort Lincoln, Griffith Park, Minidoka, Poston, Rohwer, Tule Lake), "and the only indication that this was a historical site was a metal historical marker that was pockmarked with bullet-shaped dents from locals who had apparently used it for target practice."

"There was no sign designating where the camp had once stood," Carol Mayeda continued, "we had to stop and ask some kind people if they knew where it was."

"The plaque so small and not featured in a way to stand out means that thousands of people have walked by it without bothering to stop and read it," Kathy Kojimoto SAID.

---

86. O'odham names in parentheses.

"I remember reading informational signs and feeling extremely disconnected to the experiences," said Megan Kowta (Manzanar; family in Poston) "The signs said things such as *the JA built a great community and took pride in farming fresh fruits and veggies.* I thought, *That can't be it. Who wrote this?*"

"We were given a tour of a barrack ruins and the jail that had messages written on the walls," said Willitte Hisami Ishii Herman (Tule Lake). "An abandoned bird's nest was fallen in a corner amongst a litter of blown leaves."

"I felt like a detective, searching every photo and document on display for traces of my grandmother," Miko Charbonneau continued.

"We were trying to find a trace, this missing piece of our parents, to discover a life we did not fathom," Willitte Hisami Ishii Herman continued. "Could we stir and prod old ashes for a spark, could we raise a dust devil, a wraith, of who they were back then?"

"It was when we toured the jail and saw the writing on the walls that I felt the tremendous sadness of the ancestors," said Esther Honda (Tule Lake).

"I saw my ancestors' names on the wall and I broke out in tears," said Suzanne Kimiko Onodera (Manzanar).

"I started crying as we started to drive up," Emily Mitamura continued.

"We parked and looked at the guard station," said Brian Nishimoto (Manzanar). "My mother kept saying *I think your grandfather helped build the station.* From what I can remember, my father didn't want to get out of the car."

"I remember getting back into the car," said Kelly Shimoda (Fort Missoula; family also in Heart Mountain and Poston), "and asking my father how it made him feel to go there and see everything. I remember him being silent and not having a response."

"I remember being surprised at it all because it wasn't really clear to me that my grandfather had been incarcerated," Kelly Shimoda continued. "I remember looking at a photo of him hanging on the wall. He was dressed up for a play. The photo seemed to play into the story my family always told about him having *fun* there."

"I'll never forget the experience of eating our McDonald's lunches in the mess hall," said Lisa Doi (Manzanar; family in Amache, Crystal City, Lordsburg, Rohwer). "Not sure if we were in some really fucked-up piece of performance art."

"There is something spiritually painful about stepping foot on those lands," said Sara Onitsuka (Tule Lake).

"I felt very unsettled, like the environment was steeped in bitterness," said Lauren Sumida (Jerome; family in Amache, Fort Missoula, Rohwer, Tule Lake, Tuna Canyon). "Something felt unresolved in the air."

"There is a silence that dominates the space now," said Natalie Kimura (Topaz; family also in Manzanar).

"I could hear the silence," said Julie Abo (Tule Lake; family also in Fort Richardson, Santa Fe, Lordsburg, Minidoka).

"We saw stars above the ruins," Koji Lau-Ozawa continued.

JAPANESE AMERICAN
HISTORICAL PLAZA

THE THIRD TIME I VISITED THE JAPANESE AMERICAN
Historical Plaza, a woman was shouting at a young girl. The woman was wearing a purple shirt and light blue skirt and was carrying a dozen backpacks fluttering with trinkets. She looked like a Christmas tree. The young girl, wearing a coat and an identification tag, was carved into one of the columns at the entrance to the plaza. She returned the woman's stare.

Carved into the columns: families being forced off Bainbridge Island, the first community to be removed, March 30, 1942. An old man carrying a child on his shoulders: Torazo Sakawye and his grandson Walter, photographed by Dorothea Lange, July 2, 1942. (Most captions say: "Grandfather and grandson in Manzanar.") Torazo died shortly after, "more or less of a broken heart," said Walter, who was not yet two when the photograph was taken.[87] The young girl: Miyuki Mochida, waiting for the bus to take her and her family from Hayward to Tanforan, also by Lange, May 8, 1942. (The original caption says: "Identification tags are used

---

87. Quoted in Dean Takahashi, Japanese American Internment Revisited, *Alta Journal*, October 28, 2019: altaonline.com/dispatches/a5711/internment-revisited/

to aid in keeping the family unit intact.") No names or dates appear on the columns or anywhere in the park.

Among the many places where Miyuki Mochida has been memorialized: at the entrance of the Topaz Museum's core exhibition; in a bronze statue at Tanforan; in Allen Say's *Home of the Brave*; on the cover of Susan Kamei's *When Can We Go Back to America?*; as the title image of the documentary *Guilty By Reason of Race* (1972); on the cover of Maisie and Richard Conrat's *Executive Order 9066*, her family cropped out, so that only Miyuki remains, a cover that artist Scott Tsuchitani parodied in a mock book cover for *Execrative Order 90666*, subtitled *An Ongoing Intervention into Archival Authority, Moral Certainty, Mass Melancholy, and the Collectivization of Memory, vis à vis the Japanese American Intercultural Condition*. The image is zoomed out so that Miyuki's sister Hiroko can be seen, except Hiroko's face has been replaced with the face of Hello Kitty.

In another artwork, "For the Sake of the Children," Tsuchitani transformed Miyuki and Hiroko into a carnival-style plywood cut-out, with a hole in place of Miyuki's face that people could stick their faces through. Miyuki, painted with purple coat and light blue pants, is much taller than a child. Only an adult could stick their face through, to, as Tsuchitani writes, "actively implicate themselves in the harmful normative logic that 'tone-polices' Japanese American representation in emotionally stunted ways 'for the sake of the children.'"[88] Hiroko's head does not have a hole, and she is not Hello Kitty, but Hajime, the younger brother in *Tensai Bakabon*.

I saw this installation at Rhythmix Cultural Works in Alameda, California. Tsuchitani wanted it to be interactive, for people to be able to stick their faces through the hole, but the curator thought it would be manipulative to have

---

88. Scott Tsuchitani, For the Sake of the Children artist statement, 2012

children, despite not being tall enough, stick their faces through without understanding the meaning of what they were doing, so the installation was pushed against a window. That the curator defied the artist's and the installation's requirements to avoid the potential manipulation of a child became, for me, part of the artwork. It was confrontational yet mischievous, a critique of the curatorial impulse towards empathy. I squeezed between the plywood and window and stuck my face through the hole. Yumi was running around the gallery. She was wearing a Hello Kitty T-shirt, pandemic-themed: Hello Kitty masked, surrounded by pills. What did Miyuki know or understand of her situation on May 8, 1942? What identity was she being forced to put herself through?

In *Guilty By Reason of Race*, Miyuki, in her late 30s, walks down a hallway into a gallery where Lange's photo of her (with her family once again cropped out) is mounted on a black wall. Miyuki is dressed in white. She walks toward her younger self—a woman appealing to her younger self for guidance, a young girl appealing to her older self for redemption. "Now it is possible for a defendant to look back," says the male voiceover, "to see herself across thirty years, back in that peculiar time when she was tried." Except she was not a defendant, she was not tried. Miyuki in white standing in front of Miyuki in black: an angel come back from the afterlife. "It's me on that picture," Miyuki says, "but the memories don't come."

"Do you remember reading a book about this in elementary school?" a woman asked her friend. They were in an art gallery, staring into a vitrine of small wooden birds. The gallery was filled with objects, utilitarian and art, made in camp: paintings, flowers of shells, geta, dolls, a four-foot steamship made of metal and wood.[89] The woman's question suggested the source of awareness was not a person or people, but a book, one written for children.

Everything was handmade, of salvaged materials. The birds—intricately painted, on tiny branches, some in flight, wings like waves—were made of scrap wood. I stared into their charming yet gelid, inscrutable eyes, until they were nothing but sad, solemn habits of paint, then I stared until the sadness and solemnity revealed a sentience that disarmed then depressed me.

"My mom used to have this little wooden carved bird, that was inside her jewelry box," Rea Tajiri says in *History and Memory*. A reddish-brown bird with a bright, penetrating eye, appears against a black background. The camera zooms in. "I used to ask her if I could play with it, but she kept saying, *No No No, Grandma gave me that, put that back!*

At the entrance to the gallery was a butsudan. Open, to permit the comings and goings of the spirits. It was set into a tokonoma-like alcove inside the front doors. Most people who entered walked past it. A card on the wall said it belonged to Shizue Sato Nagao, that she carried it with her when she immigrated to the United States in 1918, and later to Manzanar. She was a picture bride, the card told us, which added an aura of sympathy to the butsudan. It looked like it had something to say, in a language that depended on the forbearance of whoever was standing before it. It sat on a pedestal low to the floor. To face it directly, one had to bend down, or crouch. Also on the card was a question: "How would you choose what to bring?" How dare you, I thought, invite people who already have all the choices to pretend contemplating what choice they would make in the midst of being deprived of any choice at all.

---

89. Something From Nothing, Thacher Gallery, University of San Francisco, August-November 2017

The director of the gallery, a white woman, stood in front of the steamship and introduced the exhibition. The people in the gallery, holding plastic cups of white wine, formed a circle around her. The objects, the director said, were "proof of hope, resilience, resistance." Then she invoked the two phrases, so often repeated, that simultaneously located the exhibition, and diffused, in the guise of sharpening, its meaning: "Never forget" and "We must not let this happen again." I noticed, when she said it, six elders sitting on a bench in a corner of the gallery. It was late summer, but all six were wearing winter coats. They looked like children at a bus stop. Not exactly abandoned, not exactly looked after. When the director called everyone's attention to their presence—that there were survivors among us—there was a gasp, then everyone clapped, both sounds issuing from the shock of realizing, or being reminded, that incarceration was not as long ago as even the exhibition was forcing it to seem. Everyone looked around the gallery and stared at whoever looked old enough.

"While history functions much more smoothly in the absence of survivors, and survivors are often dissenting voices to history's narratives, history making also accords to them a very particular authority as the embodiment of authentic experience," writes Marita Sturken, in "Absent Images of Memory." The way everyone applauded the six elders without being able to find them felt like the exhibition's most moving, accurate work. The applause ended, the director concluded her remarks, and everyone returned to the exhibition.

Among the objects on display in *Then They Came for Me: Incarceration of Japanese Americans during World War II*— an exhibition of photographs by Toyo Miyatake, James Numata, Hikaru Carl Iwasaki, Roy Koyama, also Dorothea

Lange, Ansel Adams[90]—was an article in *LIFE* magazine, December 22, 1941: "How To Tell Japs From The Chinese." It included photographs of a Chinese public servant, a Japanese "warrior," a Chinese journalist, two "tall" Chinese brothers, and two "short" Japanese admirals, with descriptions of each to help readers distinguish "friendly Chinese" from "enemy alien Japs."[91] Anthropologists were consulted and determined that the Chinese face was composed of "patrician lines," was "delicately boned," with noses more "finely bridged," while the Japanese face was "massively boned," with a "pug" or "blob" nose, and showed the "humorless intensity of ruthless mystics." That line made me laugh out loud. Everyone in the gallery turned to look at me. I had seen the article before, but was struck this time by the prematurity of it being presented as an artifact. The exhibition seemed eager to present evidence of a kind of racism that had gone extinct—evidence that it had—but the article was presenting an attitude that had not gone anywhere.

One of the things most often said about the murder in Detroit, in 1982, of Vincent Chin, a twenty-seven-year-old Chinese American draftsman, is that his murderers, two white men, mistook him for Japanese. Ronald Ebens and his stepson, Michael Nitz, worked in the auto industry. The story is that Nitz was out of work, but in fact he and Ebens were both working—Nitz at a furniture store, Ebens as the foreman at an auto factory. The story of their joblessness helped to facilitate another lie: that, having been laid off, the men blamed the Japanese for destroying the American auto industry. They were already angry the night of the murder—which began at a strip club and ended in the parking lot of a McDonald's—when an Asian man entered

90. International Center of Photography, New York City, January 26, 2018–May 6, 2018

91. "How To Tell Japs From The Chinese," *LIFE*, December 22, 1941, pp. 81–82

their field of view. "It's because of you motherfuckers that we're out of work," Ebens is said to have shouted. The story is that they thought Vincent Chin was Japanese, that it was a case of mistaken identity. But the terrible logic of that story is that if Vincent Chin was Japanese, then his murder would have least corresponded with his murderers' rage; that they got the wrong guy, and that there was, therefore, a right guy. Ebens and Nitz knew that Vincent Chin was Chinese, told passersby to "get the Chinese."[92]

One implication of the *LIFE* article is that people like Ebens and Nitz, confused, allegedly, about whom to assault, would have benefited from being able to distinguish between Asian faces, as if the distinguishing features were fact, not fantasy; that the article was a field guide for white supremacists. People in the gallery were standing in small groups, looking not at the photographs, but each other. It felt more like the photographs, the people in them, were looking at the people in the gallery. There was bereavement on the faces, a shade of realizing that they had been curated onto a wall in the unfathomable future, and left there.

Near the six elders on the bench was a round table with a small collection of books, including Delphine Hirasuna's *The Art of Gaman* and Allen Eaton's *Beauty Behind Barbed Wire*. I picked up Jane Dusselier's *Artifacts of Loss*, about objects, utilitarian and art, made in camp, and flipped through pictures of furniture, jewelry, sculpture, flowers, until page 128, when I stopped and looked up. The people sparkled. Got blurry. I looked down. The image on page 128 was a photograph of a beheaded corpse. Why, in a book about art, was there a picture of a beheaded corpse? I said

92. Helen Zia, *The Vincent Chin Legacy Guide: Asian Americans Building a Movement*, Vincent and Lily Chin Estate, VincentChin.org

it out loud. I thought the corpse did too. It burned a hole in the book and in the exhibition out of which emerged what seemed to be, in the plainness of its presentation, the most revealing example of what, in the camps, was being crafted: disembodiment. The caption read: "Some Japanese Americans were driven to suicide by their internment experience." Nothing else about the corpse, or the person it belonged to, was mentioned.

A body is lying across train tracks. It looks stuffed, like a scarecrow. Misshapen, deflated. Its head has been severed, is in the shadow of the rail. The body is stretched down the slope from the tracks, legs in the dirt. A hat and a coat, folded, are a yard up the tracks. The right arm is resting on a tie, hand clenched in a fist: steeling itself for the force of the train. The face cannot be seen. There is hair, sunlight on what looks like an ear, maybe a cheek. The absence of blood placates, momentarily, the wish that the head severed from its body is an illusion. Although it takes a moment to understand what, in the photograph, is being looked at, it is clear: a man committed suicide by placing his neck on the rail.

There are fifty-three illustrations in *Artifacts of Loss*, mostly of objects—furniture, jewelry, sculpture, flowers, ikebana, kobu, bon-kei; also barrack scenes, people gardening, ice-skating. The first is a photograph by Dorothea Lange of a woman inside a horse stall. She can be seen through an open doorway, sitting behind a bed. Carved into a piece of wood hanging outside the doorway is the name Konda. The caption reads, coldly: "Living unit in Tanforan," and fails to acknowledge the woman's name. Asako Mary Konda, Nisei from California, was 29 when she was incarcerated with her brother Harry and their father Kumataro in Tanforan. The photograph is not a portrait of Asako Mary Konda though, but a statement of a condition, which the photograph reinforces. (Four years earlier, Lange took a photograph of another woman framed in a doorway of a similarly spare construction, except that she—wife of a migrant laborer, mother of three, white—has not been made uncomfortable by the camera, nor is she lost in the enforcement of namelessness, but is named, imbued with an agency withheld from Konda.) (In Tokio Ueyama's painting *The Evacuee*, which he made in Amache, a woman sits in a folding chair in the open doorway of her barrack, crocheting. Her back is to the doorway, which is framed by blue and pink curtains tied back. Outside, tarpaper barracks in the sun, a bright green tree above the roofs. The woman looks relaxed, yet focused. "Neither happy nor distraught," writes Karin Higa, "she simply exists."[93])

The forty-fourth illustration in *Artifacts of Loss* is of the beheaded corpse. It appears in a chapter titled "Mental Landscapes of Survival," in which the subject of suicide is confined to the caption, and two paragraphs. The first mentions the presence of "suicidal feelings." The second mentions the suicide of Hideo Murata, an Issei from Pismo Beach.[94] Beyond a cursory look at incarceration's threat to mental health, there is an odd lack of care for those who were unable to survive. Unlike the handmade artifacts, the man on the tracks is not endowed with a feeling of kinship

---

93. Karin Higa, "The View from Within: Japanese American Art from the Internment Camps, 1942-1945," *Hidden in Plain Sight: Selected Writings of Karin Higa.*
94. Murata shot himself in the head. Or ingested strychnine. Accounts vary. He checked himself into the Olson Hotel in Pismo Beach on a Thursday and was found dead Friday morning. A Certificate of Honorary Citizenship was found in his pocket. It was awarded for his service in WWI, and read: "Our flag was assaulted and you gallantly took up its defense." One account, which appears in Albert Marrin's *Uprooted: The Japanese American Experience During World War II*, erases the forms of resistance with which incarceration was met: "Everything went smoothly, with military precision. There were no protests or demonstrations. Nobody died, except for two Issei who committed suicide out of despair." False, false, and false.

149

or empowerment, nor with martyrdom, but estrangement, neglect. The fact that he is not named makes of his corpse an illustration.

John Yoshida, 23, was kibei, born in the United States, educated as a child in Japan. He was incarcerated in Jerome with his father, stepmother, and sister. (His mother committed suicide when he was two.) He disappeared on a Sunday. His father filed a missing person report on Monday. He was found at on Tuesday morning, 1½ miles north of camps.

"A few grew desperate, and took their own lives," says Estelle Ishigo, against the backdrop of John Yoshida's body, in Steven Okazaki's film *Days of Waiting* (1991). There are at least five additional photographs of Yoshida, all in the Bancroft Library, Berkeley. Each is of the same scene, taken from a different angle, each disclosing a new detail: two cars parked head to head on the other side of the tracks, a paper cup wedged beneath the rail, a small pond of ice, a white man in a black overcoat standing six feet away, his arms long and awkward, one of his hands an oversize talon. Yoshida's body looks, from each angle, more deflated, his head more misshapen. The act of looking grinds Yoshida's body further into the tracks.

A note, in Japanese, was found in his pocket. It was translated and published in the Jerome newspaper, the *Denson Communiqué*: "I am writing this before I die. If I cannot accomplish what I want, I am going to where my mother and grandmother are."

THE NAKAMOTO GROUP

THREE DAYS BEFORE THANKSGIVING, ON NOVEMBER 25, 2019, two yonsei activists and descendants of incarceration, Linda Sachiko Morris and Lauren Sumida, visited the offices of the Nakamoto Group in Washington, DC. They were hoping to meet with the CEO, Jennifer Nakamoto—also yonsei, also a descendant of incarceration—to deliver a petition calling for the termination of her company's contract with Immigration and Customs Enforcement (ICE). The Nakamoto Group, a private, for-profit company, was contracted to conduct annual inspections of approximately 120 of ICE's migrant detention facilities, and it had been called out, by everyone from immigrant rights groups to the Department of Homeland Security, for its failure to properly do so, the consequences of which were the increasingly fatal conditions of migrant detention in the United States.

Morris and Sumida, representing Tsuru for Solidarity, were joined by activists from Sanctuary DMV and 18 Million Rising.[95] They arrived at the second floor of a

---

95. From the Tsuru for Solidarity website, tsuruforsolidarity.org: *Tsuru for Solidarity is a nonviolent, direct action project of Japanese American social justice advocates and allies working to end detention sites and support directly impacted immigrant and refugee communities that are being targeted*

nondescript office building carrying eight banker's boxes, each containing the names of 1,000 signatories to the petition, and several envelopes containing statements prepared by other Japanese American community organizations, including Nikkei Progressives, the Japanese Community Youth Council, Densho, and Nikkei Resisters.

They were making this visit on behalf of the community, and were carrying, with their petition, the force of its collective experience. It could be considered that the community, however widespread and evolving it is, and however painful it might be to accept, included Jennifer Nakamoto. Her maternal grandparents were incarcerated in Poston. Her mother was born there. In an alternate universe, Nakamoto might have been the one visiting someone else in the community by whom she felt betrayed. Because even though Morris's and Sumida's visit was an action against an operative of the state, and against, through that operative, state violence, the nature and the energy of the visit was that of family members staging an intervention, appealing to another family member from the heart of a shared trauma, in an attempt to bring them back from the underworld.

---

by racist, inhumane immigration policies. We stand on the moral authority of Japanese Americans who suffered the atrocities and legacy of U.S. concentration camps during WWII and we say, "Stop Repeating History!"

From the Sanctuary DMW website, sanctuarydmv.org: *Sanctuary DMV is a feminist, anti-imperialist, all-volunteer group standing in solidarity with immigrants and marginalized communities in the DMV area (DC, Maryland, and Virginia). We resist policies and policy proposals that target and aim to deport millions of undocumented immigrants and discriminate against Black, Indigenous, Muslim, Latinx, and LGBTQ+ people.*

From the 18 Million Rising website, 18MR.org: *18MR.org was founded to promote AAPI civic engagement, influence, and movement by leveraging the power of technology and social media. Our vision of engaged AAPI communities began with, but doesn't end with, the ballot box: it also includes year-round civic activity locally and nationally, holding corporations accountable, building interracial coalitions, and developing our shared identities.*

At the time of the visit, the Nakamoto Group had been under scrutiny for its inspection practices: their preferential interview process, only interviewing people who spoke English, not Spanish or Indigenous languages; failing to report unsafe and unhealthy conditions; failing to report a lack of medical and mental health care; failing to report sexual assaults; failing to report the overuse of solitary confinement.

In June 2018, DHS released a report finding that the Nakamoto Group "misrepresented the work performed in evaluating the actual conditions of the facilities"; that the inspectors were "not always thorough," were often unable to complete inspections, and conducted inconsistent and insufficient interviews. In November 2018, eleven Senators wrote a letter to Nakamoto calling out the Nakamoto Group for these misrepresentations and demanding information about the company's contracts and procedures.[96] In September 2019, Congress held a hearing to examine whether DHS was "doing enough" (Congress's words) to oversee the conditions of ICE detention facilities. They called on Nakamoto to testify.

These were among the official calls for accountability. But none of them were appealing from a position of solidarity with the migrants or from the belief that the migrant detention facilities should not be reformed, but be shut down and abolished, and none of them were as significant and searing as Morris's and Sumida's, because none of them were appealing, from the specificity of a shared experience, to the conscience of Nakamoto herself.

Morris's and Sumida's visit was livestreamed. Laura Li, representing 18 Million Rising, recorded. The five activists

<hr>

96. Elizabeth Warren, Ron Wyden, Kamala Harris, Kirsten Gillibrand, Richard Blumenthal, Bernie Sanders, Cory Booker, Ed Markey, Mazie Hirono, Tom Udall, Jeff Merkley.

emerged from an elevator and carried their boxes down a hallway to Suite 240. On the wall inside the door was an enormous fan with two goddesses riding a dragon above a sea of waves. On top of a file cabinet was a geisha doll. "Interesting décor," Li said. The office—drop-panel ceiling, empty file trays on a sideboard, no windows—looked fake. In the center was a desk, a black computer, a canister of WD-40, and a call bell. Morris rang it.

A woman appeared from behind a wall. "Yes?" she said, in a tone that suggested she knew why they were there, but was pretending, hard, that she did not. Morris introduced the groups, the reason they were there, and asked if Naka-moto was in.

"No," the woman said.

"Is there anyone who can speak on her behalf?"

"No. It's the holiday week, they're all out."

"Would we be able to speak to you?"

When Morris explained that they were delivering a petition calling for the Nakamoto Group to end its con-tracts with ICE, the woman began calculating her way out of the room. "Give me one second," she said, then dis-appeared.

While they waited, Sumida turned to the livestream: "We're hoping to be able to deliver not only the petition but approximately 200 paper cranes, which were folded in mem-ory of all those who have died in ICE custody. We are hoping that the Nakamoto Group will be able to accept these cranes as a first step to hold themselves accountable for being com-plicit in mass incarceration and abuses of immigrants."

Five minutes passed. Morris rang the bell again. Six min-utes. A large man appeared from behind the wall, and stood at the edge of the room. "Hi, can I help you?" he asked. Morris introduced the groups again, explained that they had a petition and statements they wanted to deliver to Nakamoto, and asked that if she was not in, could they leave them with the man or the woman, or on the desk?

The man offered so many excuses—"No one's here who can accept them," "I work here part-time," "I'm on a tight deadline"—that it seemed as if he did not want the visitors to leave, but enjoyed their company.

Finally, he threatened to call the cops. He did not brandish a phone though, or make a move toward one, but continued to stand there, hands in pockets. The woman returned. Morris asked why they could not simply leave the petition and the statements on the desk. When it seemed that the impasse was not going to hold any longer, Sumida, holding the tsuru, spoke:

"We came here carrying a lot of pain from other members of our community." They spoke plaintively, holding back tears. "We just wanted a chance to be able to share what Ms. Nakamoto has done. It's unacceptable to our community. The way that she has used her history is disgusting. And we wanted this place, this space, to speak on behalf of our community. From what happened to us and our families during WWII, being incarcerated in the camps, forced out of their homes, their businesses. My grandfather couldn't keep going to school. His father was arrested after Pearl Harbor and taken to a Department of Justice camp." It was the first moment, in the office, in which a family member was invoked, in which the potential abstraction of the past was clarified in the invocation of a person, *my grandfather*.

"I don't know what that has to do with our contract," the woman said, "but you gotta go."

Morris intervened. "During her congressional testimony, Ms. Nakamoto spoke specifically about her family's history of incarceration during WWII. She invoked that history and that is not just her history. That history belongs to us. That history belongs to our community."

The desk in the center of the room reminded me of a desk I had seen in an exhibition in the Presidio, San Francisco:

a replica of the desk of John DeWitt, commanding general of the Western Defense Command, which was formed in March 1941 to control the Pacific coast. [97] "A Jap's a Jap," DeWitt infamously said. "It makes no difference whether he is an American citizen or not." The desk was on an elevated platform in the center of the main gallery, a monstrously illuminated fetish object. This, I thought, of the Nakamoto Group's desk, is what a desk looks like prior to becoming a museum piece, when it is still in the midst of its violence: inconspicuous, mundane, a little downcast, disheveled. I imagined it becoming the centerpiece, and the black hole, of a future exhibition, one highlighting—while commemorating—the early twenty-first century phase of the unending tradition of migrant detention in the United States.

Jennifer Nakamoto spoke before the House Homeland Security Subcommittee on Oversight and Management on September 26, 2019. Her microphone was off. A man leaned in to turn it on. "Sorry," Nakamoto whispered, five times. "Sorry, sorry, sorry, sorry." She introduced the Nakamoto Group as a "woman-owned, minority-owned, small, disadvantaged business," although she did not clarify the meaning of "small" or "disadvantaged." From 2015 to 2019, the Nakamoto Group received $22,538,084 from ICE, and had just received from them, shortly before the hearing, an additional $3,738,177.

"My great-grandparents immigrated to the United States from Japan," she said. "My maternal grandparents were born in California, making them United States citizens.

97. *Exclusion: The Presidio's Role in World War II Japanese American Incarceration*, Presidio Officers' Club Heritage Gallery, San Francisco, April 2017–March 2018

After Pearl Harbor, the Presidential Order was issued to incarcerate all Japanese, regardless of their citizenship status. My maternal family were living in California and had to relinquish all of their property including any businesses that they had. They were given one trash bag to fill of personal items to take with them and had to leave everything else behind. Our family was spread out to various internment camps across the country. My maternal grandparents were incarcerated in a Japanese internment camp in Arizona. They were there long enough to meet, fall in love, get married, have a baby—my mother."

After sharing her family's story, Nakamoto recounted the origins of the Nakamoto Group, which she started in 2003. She did not seem embattled or ashamed, only ill-prepared. Her answers to questions regarding basic information about the Nakamoto Group's practices were confused. She turned around several times to look at someone in the gallery. She ended several answers mid-sentence, did not answer some questions at all. "What is the value of your current contracts with ICE?" "When do your current contracts expire?" "How many days' notice do you provide detention facilities prior to an inspection?" "Sixty," she said. She turned around to the gallery, then said, "Thirty." Rep. Dan Crenshaw asked if she could give an example of a "life safety" issue, which was one of the areas of inspection she mentioned. She could not. She admitted that she did not know the health and safety standards "by heart." Rep. Dina Titus cited the statistic that during a year-and-a-half span, migrants had been put in solitary confinement 121 times, 16 of which lasted 75 days. She asked Nakamoto if she could explain the difference between solitary confinement and segregation. She could not.

"It wasn't until I watched her face simple questions that I got a sense of her full betrayal," wrote Sharon Yamato in

Rafu Shimpo.[98] "It seemed she decided it might be helpful to use her Japanese American heritage to try to make us forget why she was there and to give the impression that she's somehow connected to the immigrants she's responsible for protecting."

"I was shaking," Morris told me. "I was so upset in the office that I felt like my face was..." she touched her cheeks... "contorting. I felt like everything in my body was just...coming up, all of the pain and trauma coming up, in that office. I think there was probably a part of me that was afraid that I wouldn't be able to say the things that I needed to say. I really wanted to be powerful and strong, but my whole body was just like, *No, no, no, no, no...*"

When Morris was in college, she took an Asian American Studies class. On the first day, when her professor asked everyone to introduce themselves, she said, "I'm half Japanese," to which her professor said, "Why only half?" Morris, who grew up outside of DC and attended a high school where she was the only Japanese American, did not know how to respond. She had never been asked that question before.

She told her class that her family was incarcerated during WWII, that her grandparents met and married in camp, but that she had been told not to ask questions about it. "I remember my parents warning me that any reminder of camp would potentially set my grandmother off," Morris told me, "and then she would shut down for days, weeks. I think I probably learned not to ask about it before I learned what camp was." It was the beginning of her understanding of what camp meant, of how its meaning was not historical, but present, and its presence was pain, which burned

98. Sharon Yamato, "Who Is Jenni Nakamoto?" Rafu Shimpo, 12/11/2019

into Morris's sense of identity. "I knew there was a lot of intense trauma and shame around it. And I think the shame was the biggest thing that stuck with me because that's the thing that I think I inherited. It was just so clear to me that being Japanese American was very loaded, with a lot of grief, and a lot of self-hatred."

Her professor gave her the assignment of talking to her grandmother, as if the silence would be dispelled by the mandate of a school assignment. Morris called her grandmother. She asked a few introductory questions, about details, mostly, which her grandmother answered without emotion. The call lasted ten minutes, maybe fifteen.

"There's a big part of me that hoped that if we could be in a room with her, that we would be able to connect," Morris said, about Nakamoto. "The thing that her family went through is the thing that our family went through, and even her actions—using our history to try to justify this terrible thing that she's doing—I know where that comes from. We were coming there to call her out, but we were also coming there as community." Nakamoto had become emblematic of a kind of assimilation that Anne Anlin Cheng describes, in *The Melancholy of Race*, as "the repetition of a violence (against an other that is also the self) that she has already experienced."

The activists carried the boxes and petitions and statements and tsuru out of the office. They left the building and gathered on the sidewalk to give their final statements to the livestream. Sumida spoke directly to Nakamoto: "Your use of your history to shield yourself is a betrayal. You have a lot of healing to do for yourself and for the harm you have caused."

I remember thinking how generous "healing" sounded. That despite the betrayal and the harm that Nakamoto was causing, Sumida demanded that she find a way to heal. "Healing" evoked, in my mind, a long, arduous, ultimately affirming process through which Nakamoto might nurture herself and her ancestors—bruised, perhaps, by the perverse and brutal reality of their future in Nakamoto's work—to a place of health. Because the person who has fallen farthest from community might still be considered a member of that community, and one worth saving.

JAPANESE AMERICAN
HISTORICAL PLAZA

THE FOURTH TIME I VISITED THE JAPANESE AMERICAN Historical Plaza, I heard shouting. Someone was shouting for help, or maybe they were delivering a speech. Maybe there were two people, shouting at each other. When I reached the sound, a man was moving in a wide circle around the tall stone inscribed with the names of the ten camps. He was wearing jeans, a black button-down shirt, and was barefoot. A pair of black high-tops were placed very neatly on the ground facing the stone. The man's shouting rose and fell. He got down on his hands and knees and crawled to the shoes, slipped his hands into them and slapped the ground. Sat cross-legged in front of the stone. Threw himself on the ground, thrust his right leg in the air, waved it around. Sat up and slapped the ground again. His shouts were swallowed by the sound of traffic, a train, a dog barking near the river. He put his face to the ground, like he was going to kiss it. Then he stood up, slipped the shoes off his hands, and ran into the city.

I had become accustomed to the Japanese American Historical Plaza being a place for people in distress. And I had become accustomed to the indifference of the people who pretended they could not see or hear any of that. Maybe it was better that no one was paying attention to the man. It gave space to his episode in a way that enabled him to see it through. The Japanese American Historical Plaza had achieved the unexpected purpose of providing a space where people could fall apart.

A few blocks away in a black box theater, *Hold These Truths*, a play by Jeanne Sakata, starring Ryun Yu as Gordon Hirabayashi, ran for forty-five nights. Hirabayashi, Nisei from Seattle, was a senior at the University of Washington when he refused the curfew enforced by the Western Defense Command, March 1942. The curfew was in effect 8 p.m. to 6 a.m. He also refused to register for the forced removal, instead turning himself in to the FBI. He was arrested; he challenged his arrest, all the way to the Supreme Court. He lost, and was sent to prison. (Forty years later, his convictions were vacated.) Not only did Yu play Hirabayashi, he played all of the people in Hirabayashi's life—family and friends, allies and enemies. And he played them *as* Hirabayashi. That is a condition we share: holding in our heads all the people we know by inventing them over and over. Seeing Yu as Hirabayashi as both himself and everyone else clarified the porousness of being a subject indentured to tell and retell the story of their erasure against the ongoing force of their being erased. The performance was not an homage to the triumph of Americanism, but a nightmarish dance for which, even in the afterlife, there was no possibility of escape.

The theater was full. The audience was white and old. It was not a stretch to imagine them as children, watching their friends and neighbors take their houses apart. They sat on three sides of the stage. There were three chairs. Depending on how Yu arranged them, they denoted walls, rooms, spaces of interrogation, detention. A game of musical chairs played alone. Yu rarely stopped moving. He was sweating, his nose started running. He had a handkerchief, incorporated it seamlessly, but his nose would not stop running.[99] At one point, he entered the audience. It felt precarious. I was afraid that if Yu fell over, Hirabayashi would land in the lap of a stranger, lose his place, and have to start his life over again.

On May 13, 1942, Ichiro Shimoda, a 45-year-old gardener from Los Angeles, was shot and killed by guards at Fort Sill. An FBI memo dated five days later reads: "One Jap became mildly insane and was placed in the military hospital. Shimoda attempted to escape at 7:30 a.m. He climbed the first fence, ran down the runway, and started to climb the second fence, when he was shot and killed by two shots, one entering the back of his head."

A day earlier, on May 12, Kanesaburo Oshima, a general store owner from Hawaii, was shot and killed by guards, also at Fort Sill. According to Yoshitaro Amano, a Japanese Panamanian, "Oshima ran between the barbed wire fences and threw himself halfway up the outer gate but the overhanging barbed wire stopped him. Even if no one did a thing to stop him, Oshima wouldn't have succeeded. We shouted, *Don't shoot. He's crazy!* The guard shot him from three meters away. Oshima dropped. The medics said a second shot went through his head."[100]

Oshima immigrated from Nagano, where his parents were silkworm farmers, to Hawaii, where he worked on a sugar plantation. When his contract ended, he moved to Kona. He married a young woman, Matsu, also from

---

99. "He seemed to have a cold and was dripping sweat from the lights," said Janice Akemi Nabeta Schell, who saw the play on a different night in a different place: San Diego, December 8, 2019. "I thought, Oh no, he might really be crying or maybe he's sick! It did almost seem like it was part of the performance. It made me feel more sympathy for the character, as if the actor was feeling the story so deeply."
100. Yoshitaro Amano, *The Journal of My Incarceration* (Tokyo, 1943)

a silkworm family in Nagano. They had twelve children. Oshima worked as a cook, a barber, in a movie theater (silent movies), and as a taxi driver. Of his general store, former customers remembered especially the pastries, red reef fish, and ice cream. According to his son Susumu, Oshima volunteered at the Japanese consulate helping Issei fill out paperwork (marriage licenses, birth and death certificates). Susumu guessed that was why his father was detained by the FBI immediately after Pearl Harbor. He was sent from Kilauea to Sand Island to 801 Silver Avenue to Fort Sill. He cut prisoners' hair to make money to buy paper to write letters to his family.

According to Gary Okihiro's *Encyclopedia of Japanese American Internment*, Oshima "constantly worried over their wellbeing." Also according to the *Encyclopedia of Japanese American Internment*, "Shimoda worried over the fate of his wife and family back in Los Angeles, and was thus depressed."

Much less is known about Shimoda. He was taken from his family the night of December 7, 1941, and sent to Fort Missoula. On the train, he tried to bite off his tongue. At Fort Missoula, he tried to asphyxiate himself. He was written up as mentally unstable. He was transferred to Fort Sill in March 1942. The administration, including the guards, were made aware of his psychological state, and that he was not a threat to anyone but himself.

He appears in a poem: "May 1942" by Mariko Nagai:

Today, rumor has it,
a Japanese man was shot
to death as he tried
to escape from a camp
in Oklahoma, or was it Montana?
His name was Ichiro Shimoda.

Ichiro, the first son.[101]

Oshima also appears in a poem: "Winter Letter to San Francisco" by Brian Komei Dempster:

Right
outside the barrack, a line of us dropped
back against the wall. Oshima-san ran, floodlights
    brushing
his face gold. He climbed the fence
until chrome plugs wilted him in the eye
of the light, back slapping the ice shadows.[102]

According to JANM's Chronology of WWII Incarceration, Shimoda was the first to be murdered. No mention is made, in the same chronology, of Oshima. According to the Densho Encyclopedia's entry on homicides in camp, Oshima was the first. No mention is made, in the same entry, of Shimoda.

According to Yoshitaro Amano, Shimoda was not shot and killed by guards at Fort Sill, but suffered a nervous breakdown after witnessing Oshima's murder: "He was removed to a tent and his friends took turns watching over him. The soldiers heard about this and said they'd take care of him. We thought the army regretted killing Oshima and were trying to make amends. How naïve. Four days later, on May 24, we were notified of Shimoda's death. He had been a very powerful man and I saw him as he was taken away. He couldn't have died naturally in four or five days. His death was suspicious. We asked to see his body but were denied and soldiers reported that he had already been embalmed."[103]

---

101. Mariko Nagai, "May 1942," *Dust of Eden* (Park Ridge, IL: Albert Whitman & Co., 2014)

102. Brian Komei Dempster, "Winter Letter to San Francisco," *Topaz* (New York: Four Way Books, 2013)

103. Yoshitaro Amano, *The Journal of My Incarceration*, op. cit.

This version of history resurrects Shimoda as a witness, and his mental instability as a consequence of having witnessed another man being killed. His nervous breakdown enfolded into it the possibility that he too was shot and killed. His mental instability and nervous breakdown were occasions for him to be sentenced, if not to death, then to be disappeared.

In Amano's memoir, Shimoda's name is not Ichiro, but Itsuji. According to an FBI memo, Itsuji Shimoda was detained in Santa Monica on December 8, 1941. According to a typewritten list in Carol Van Valkenburg's *An Alien Place: The Fort Missoula, Montana, Detention Center 1941-44*, Itsuji Shimoda was among the prisoners transferred from Fort Missoula to Fort Sill.

Kanesaburo Oshima was playing hanafuda with friends when he abruptly got up from the table, walked outside and asked the first guard he saw for an an axe. "What do you want an axe for?" "To chop wood." The guard said no. Oshima kept walking. Then started running.

Oshima's wife was sitting outside the family store in Kona when the police arrived. Susumu was at school. Somebody came to notify him. "All of a sudden I had a feeling," he said. A few days later, a death certificate arrived in the mail. It stated that Oshima died from a gunshot. A funeral, presided over by Reverend Hozui Nakayama from the Daifukuji Soto Mission Buddhist Temple in Hawaii, was held at Fort Sill. All the prisoners were in attendance. As were the guards, who, fearing revolt, kept their guns aimed at the mourners. Oshima was buried at Fort Sill. His oldest son, Noboru, later had his remains reburied in Kona. The whereabouts of Shimoda's remains are unknown.

801 SILVER AVENUE

AFTER HOM WONG SHEE

ON AUGUST 12, 1940, THE IMMIGRATION STATION ON Angel Island burned down. The cause was an electrical fire, but could it have been the angels? The immigration station was on a hill tucked into a cove, China Cove, named for the country from which a majority of the immigrants were arriving. Angel Island was named by Juan Manuel de Ayala y Aranza, Spanish explorer, and one of the first Europeans to invade San Francisco Bay. Maybe when Ayala anchored his ship off the island, he felt something, maybe even the touch of what he described, romantically, sinisterly, as an *angel*. The island is one mile square and shaped like a sting ray. For thousands of years, the Coast Miwok rowed small boats from the mainland, set up camp in the coves. They built houses of branches and bulrushes, hunted and fished, gathered acorns and greens, then dismantled their houses and erased their footprints. They were there when Ayala arrived. Ayala referred to them as "tender lambs." Those who were not enslaved were forced off the island. Those who were enslaved got sick from the white man's food, were infected by the white man's diseases, and/or died.

The immigration station was built to enforce the Chinese Exclusion Act, which was signed in 1882. The law, however, did not prevent people from arriving, but made the process of arrival more convoluted and harrowing, forcing immigrants to balance their lives, their luck and their bodies, on a knife edge. The immigration station was also a deportation facility, which contrived the keystone misunderstanding of what immigration continues to mean, especially in the white imagination, especially of those farthest removed from the realities of immigration: to arrive and to be summarily expelled, days, weeks, months later, or immediately.

Actually, only the administration building burned, which is where the women were detained, and where, awaiting the adjudication of their histories and their futures, they carved poems into the walls. Unlike the hundreds of poems carved into the walls by the men, which have been translated, published, enshrined as memorials, the poems written by the women exist only in the memory of the dead. One immigrant, Mrs. Loo, remembered "plenty of poems on the wall." Lee Puey You, an immigrant in her early twenties, remembered "the bathroom filled with sad and bitter poems."[104] The building, falling apart, embodied the contradiction of being both the frontline fortification of the nation's war on Asian immigration and completely neglected. Electrical fire? I think it was the angels. And even though that was the end of the immigration station's thirty-year reign on Angel Island, the immigration station itself was lifted out of the embers and off the island and set down on a hill across the bay in San Francisco, at 801 Silver Avenue.

801 Silver Avenue is a large brick building that houses the Cornerstone Academy, a private school, pre-K through eighth grade, run by the Cornerstone Evangelical Baptist

---

104. Erika Lee and Judy Yung, *Angel Island: Immigrant Gateway to America*, (Oxford, UK: Oxford University Press, 2012)

Church. The church was founded in 1975 by Chanson Lau, a Chinese American pastor. His bio on the church's website begins: "After accepting Jesus Christ as his personal Lord and Savior, God took Chanson on the ride of a lifetime."

The building bears the hallmarks of being fearsome and imposing—tall doorways like teeth, dark glowering windows like eye sockets, the haunted look of an asylum—but seemed, the day I visited, almost sunny. There were no shadows on its façade, unlike in black-and-white photographs, in which the building, occupied by INS, looks like it can be entered but not exited. Its sunny quality must have had something to do with it being filled with children, and the idea, even, of the busyness of their classrooms. And yet the building was quiet. Was everyone out on a field trip? Was it naptime?

I did not know, when I visited, that it was a school. Before INS, 801 Silver Avenue was home to the Training College of the Salvation Army, which went bankrupt in 1935. After the war, it was home to Simpson Bible College, a Christian missionary school. Cornerstone Academy bought the property in 1989. The purchase was made, according to their website, "by a miracle of God."

The architectural requirements of a school are apparently the same as that of a detention facility. Within three days of Pearl Harbor, nearly 100 Issei men from Northern California and the Bay Area were detained at 801 Silver Avenue. A month later, forty more were detained. A month after that, nearly 200 more, adding to a population that included German and Italian nationals, and Chinese immigrants, including women and children. The Issei were removed from their families and homes, their communities and places of work, and detained in the gymnasium. They slept on bunk beds three beds high. And awaited interrogation and eventual transfer to another detention facility: Sharp Park down the coast in Pacifica, Fort Lincoln in North Dakota, Fort Missoula in Montana, among them.

I went to 801 Silver Avenue to visit with the memory of
the Issei, and to get a sense, however atmospheric, of their
first view of the war. It was a school day, but the parking lot was empty. The lobby was small, not as grand as
the building suggested. Carpeted, with potted plants and a
small table with brochures. It felt like the foyer of a church,
which I guess it was. An Asian American woman was sitting at a reception desk. She was friendly, asked how she
could help.

"I'm visiting places where Japanese Americans were
detained during WWII," I said—straight, like a schoolchild.

The woman froze. The walls were decorated with drawings by children, their names scrawled at the bottom, all
Chinese.

"Chinese immigrants too," I said, which was true, but I
was recalculating, thinking that the woman might be more
interested in Chinese immigrants than the Issei.

"This used to be a detention center," I said.

What kind of harbinger was I? I felt embarrassed, then
ashamed, like I was forcing on the woman some terribly
negative energy. I wanted desperately to take it back.

"I don't know," she said. "I don't think so."

I sounded like I was lost and was asking for directions—
to the nearest detention center.[105] I am not sure what I was
expecting. I suppose I thought that whomever I might
encounter would let me wander the building or, more
absurdly, offer to give me a tour. Then I would have been
peeking into classrooms full of children, and how would I
explain myself then? Would I have interrupted each class

---

105. Later that day, looking for the site of Sharp Park, I got lost, dead-
ended at a golf course, and asked a woman, also Asian American, for
directions. She was wearing a pink sweater vest over a white polo shirt,
collar turned up, khaki shorts, a white visor, and was pulling clubs out of
her trunk. She was flustered, and a little scared, like I had popped out of
the trees. The ground tilted. I heard voices, then arrows.

to tell the students that their classroom was once used to detain Asian people?

My visits to incarceration sites have been intentional, but they have not been programmatic. I rarely know what I am looking for and when I find what I do not know I am looking for, I often turn away and look at something else, something that has nothing, or nothing obvious, to do with the past, but that becomes its emissary, at least that is how it feels. I am drawn especially to sites in which no trace of the past remains, or in which the past is propagated, at most, by traces.

Whenever I am getting close to these sites, I carry with me the delusion that everyone who is there—who I see and meet—is not only aware of the site and its history, but carries a piece of it with them, if they are not a piece of it themselves. The delusion is based on a simple desire: that we know where we are, which means knowing what happened there. The desire is based, in turn, on the feeling that I do not know where I am, which means that everyone who is there, even if they arrived only moments before, knows more than I do. I have met many people in the ruins of incarceration who did not know that is what happened there, and though I used to be surprised, I am increasingly confirmed in my understanding of the United States as an anti-memorial to everyone and everything it has disappeared and/or destroyed, and of its citizens as the stewards of that disappearance and destruction.

On November 19, 1941, a Chinese woman, Hom Wong Shee, committed suicide at 801 Silver Avenue. Wong Shee, 46, had been in detention with, yet separated from, her two youngest sons for twenty-five days when she drove chopsticks into her ears and cut her throat with a pocketknife. It was after midnight. Everyone was asleep. The matron on duty said that Wong Shee had, in the days before, been "acting queerly," that she had been "getting up out of bed and making noise," that she kept saying that she was going "crazy."[106]

What Wong Shee said was: "I'm at my wit's end."[107]

Wong Shee spoke Taishanese, a Cantonese dialect from Guangdong Province, the Pearl River Delta. She immigrated to the US in the 1920s. She married a businessman, Hom Hen Shew, who served with the American Expeditionary Forces in WWI. They lived in Pittsburgh and had seven children. In 1932, they returned to China, had two more children, sons, Hom Lee Min and Hom King Min. Hen Shew returned to the US, to New York, with all of the children except for the youngest sons. When Japan began bombing Guangdong, Wong Shee, Lee Min, and King Min moved to Hong Kong, then to the US to rejoin the rest of the family. They arrived in San Francisco on October 23, 1941, and were detained and separated—Shee to the women's quarters, her sons to the gymnasium. Wong Shee made repeated requests for her and her sons to be detained together, then, when those requests were denied, to at least be able to see them. Those requests were also denied, for the reason that her sons were "old enough to take care of themselves." They were eight and nine.

Wong Shee became increasingly desperate. The head matron heard high-pitched screams coming from her room, which the nurse told her was typical of Chinese women. "They sometimes act that way when disappointed," she said.[108] Wong Shee watched as other women failed their hearings and were deported, and feared the same thing happening to her and her sons. She had no money, owed debts on her return to the US, her family had not been

106. caamedia.org/separatelivesbrokendreams/chop13.html
107. caamedia.org/separatelivesbrokendreams/chop.html
108. caamedia.org/separatelivesbrokendreams/chop13.html

informed about their detention, she was suffering high blood pressure, and was hard of hearing.

Wong Shee's oldest son, Hom You Yee, a soldier in the US Army, stationed at Fort Benning, Georgia, wrote a letter to INS asking about his mother's death. A letter came back. "Inasmuch as you are a member of the same family," it began. The language was senseless. It offered no information and no condolences, but mentioned You Yee's young brothers, still in detention. "Hearings will proceed as soon as conditions permit," the letter concluded, making clear that despite their mother's death, they would receive no special attention.[109]

An investigation conducted internally by INS confirmed Wong Shee's mistreatment—the separation from her sons, her requests to be reunited with them neglected or denied, not receiving medical or mental health attention, the fact, more generally, that the staff at 801 Silver Avenue neither spoke nor understood Chinese, not to mention her dialect. It was also revealed that her mistreatment was not exceptional, that she had been treated no different than any of the Chinese immigrants at 801 Silver Avenue or any of the thousands on Angel Island, which included the fact that not only her mistreatment but the results of the investigation into her mistreatment were lost, buried in the archives, out of reach and out of consciousness.

I did not know about Hom Wong Shee when I visited 801 Silver Avenue. I was disturbed by how easily the school seemed to have consumed the history with which it shared a building. Most of the incarceration sites structures I have visited have been converted into memorials, ruins, or some uneasy combination of the two, or have been replaced by some form of American decadence or oblivion, a shopping mall (e.g., Tanforan detention center), a campground (e.g.,

---

109. caamedia.org/separatelivesbrokendreams/chop10.html

Tucson Federal Prison Camp), an archery range (e.g., Sharp Park detention center), but 801 Silver Avenue was still there on the hill. The Cornerstone Academy's mission, based on Christian principles, includes preparing students for "productive lives as responsible citizens in a free and competitive society."[110]

What do these words, individually and together, mean, and in relation to children? Wong Shee wanted to go home. She wanted her sons and she wanted the three of them to go home. Even though she had lived in, and even though she and her sons had already entered, the United States, she was being held at its border, which the war was making stronger yet more obtuse.

If I had known about Hom Wong Shee, would I have approached the building differently, or at all? An immigration station, a detention facility, an interrogation room, a gymnasium filled with beds stacked *Squid Game*–style where hundreds of men and two young boys keep or lose track of time while awaiting their fate; a room where women are kept awake by the distress of a woman kept awake by the thought of her sons on the far side of several impenetrable walls, is already a funereal space, but death changes it, deepens it, makes it irrecoverable.

There is no marker, no plaque. Until there is, if there is, I will continue to understand the memorial to the immigrants and to Hom Wong Shee to be this absence, and the comprehensive erasure of the fact that the immigrants had been there. And I will continue to understand the memorial to exist in the lack of awareness that is being passed down to the children and the form of their futures as "responsible citizens."

110. cornerstone-academy.net/mission-statement

In "A Death Diary," a poem written for her grandmother, Mia Ayumi Malhotra asks, "What is the difference between a ghost and an ancestor?"[111] Mia, sansei on her mother's side, yonsei on her father's side, had seventeen family members incarcerated during WWII—in the detention center in Stockton, in the DOJ prison in Lordsburg, in Rohwer. Who among the seventeen are ghosts and who among them are ancestors, I wondered, reading the poem. Can they each be only one? I thought of my grandfather, who might have known, in Fort Missoula, some of the men from 801 Silver Avenue. I have known my grandfather, since his death, as a ghost and as an ancestor, but I cannot say if he has been both at the same time, only that these facets—or revelations—of him and his memory do not seem incompatible, might even be inseparable. But Malhotra's question is, what is the *difference*?

I mourn the ways the dead are deprived of a place in the lives—the days and nights, thoughts and feelings—of the living. Maybe it is less about paying attention to the dead and more about sharing with the dead what we are paying attention to. Because if I were to attempt an answer to Mia's question, I would say that the difference between a ghost and an ancestor is the difference between the withholding and the sharing of our attention, that a ghost exists wherever we, the living, are not sharing our lives with the dead and that an ancestor is the definition of that sharing.

When I left the building, a group of children was lining up in the parking lot. The children, some with backpacks, some with lunch boxes, some wearing hats, all wearing white, lined up along the yellow lines. They were remarkably quiet.

111. Mia Ayumi Malhotra, "A Death Diary," *Notes from the Birth Year*, (Bar Harbor, ME: Bateau Press, 2022)

So was their teacher, a young woman. I waved, they did not wave back. I felt gangly, like an inflatable air dancer. I also felt distant, incongruous with the present, as if I had emerged not through the front door of their school, but out of an entirely different building.

The sun was bright. The children's shadows, growing out of the yellow lines and out of their feet, were soft, softly radiant at their edges, and were moving in a way that made them seem almost independent from the children, as if the children, standing still, were not casting shadows at all, but, in their innocence and lack of awareness, had let their spirits slip out of their bodies.

TO FORCE UPON THEM
THE AUTHORITY OF
HISTORY

"I REMEMBER READING A PICTURE BOOK BY A FRIEND'S uncle, *Baseball Saved Us*, when I was little," said Mia Ayumi Malhotra, "and knowing that there was something weighty about the scenes depicted in the book—the dust, the miles of desert, the grim barracks."

"I remember having books around the house, namely *Lone Heart Mountain* by Estelle Ishigo," said Melissa Ayumi Bailey.

"Nearly all of what I knew about incarceration during my childhood came from reading books, particularly by Yoshiko Uchida," said Emily Nakashima. "I remember *Journey to Topaz* and *Journey Home* most vividly."

"The first book I read on the subject was *Citizen 13660* by Miné Okubo," said Maryn Ayumi Masumiya. "Another was *The Manzanar Fishing Club*."

"My mom bought me [Yoshiko Uchida's] *The Bracelet* when I was very young," said Alexandra Arai Cauley. "I think I must have been six or seven."

"My children are five and seven and we're currently reading [Winifred Conkling's] *Sylvia & Aki*," said Jonathan Ota. "My seven-year-old has had a lot of questions—about whether being forced to move because we're Japanese is something we have to worry about."

When Jenna Nishimura was in first grade, her grandmother took her to Pearl Harbor, where she worked for over forty years, "She seemed so at home," Nishimura said. Until the USS Arizona. She became visibly uncomfortable, told Nishimura and her sister to go alone. The attendant would not let them. "She acquiesced and got on the little motor boat out to the floating memorial." Nishimura remembers looking at the water and seeing "the occasional bubble of oil that floated up and burst iridescent on the surface."

"I had my first physical reaction when reading Yoshiko Uchida's *Journey to Topaz* at age 7," said Sean Miura.

When Miko Charbonneau was in second or third grade, she learned about the Holocaust. "I raised my hand and said my grandparents were also held in camp," she said. "The teacher was flustered, and after a long pause said, *Well we didn't kill them.* I told my family and Grandma was pissed off. She gave me a big black book of Manzanar photos and told me to bring it in and give it to him."

When she was learning about WWII in fourth grade, Katherine Terumi Laubscher's classmates called her a *Jap.* "My mother was furious," she said. "She demanded my classmates apologize, and asked the teacher to explain to my classmates why what they had said was wrong. The teacher, who seemed to be very uncomfortable, assured my mother that she had spoken with them and that they were very sorry."

When Traci Oshiro was in fourth grade, her grandmother's cousin, Gordon Hirabayashi, came over. "Everyone gathered around our kitchen table listening to him speak," she said. She remembers her mom driving her to school and telling her that "Gordon was arrested for being Japanese and only recently got his record cleared."

"I didn't learn about the camps in a meaningful way until [Jeanne Wakatsuki Houston's] *Farewell to Manzanar* in fourth grade," said Emily Merolli. "I freaked out, and remember asking my dad whether he had heard of this craziness, and whether we might know anyone who had been put into the camps. He shrugged and said, *Yes, my dad and your obasan.*"

When Scott Tsuchitani was in fourth grade, his mother gave him *Journey to Topaz*. His family also had Maisie and Richard Conrat's *Executive Order 9066*, which included photographs from the National Archives. "I remember my very nearsighted father taking off his glasses to study the photos. He pointed to a photo that included TSUCHITANI in very faint letters on a list of names of families to be evacuated."

When Emily Nakashima was in fourth grade, she had to design an outfit for a character in a book related to California history. She was assigned *Journey to Topaz*. "A theme in my K12 schooling: white teachers wanted *me* to learn about Asian America history, but not necessarily everyone else."

When Amy Lee-Tai was in elementary school (1970s), her mother gave her *Journey to Topaz*. "I lay sprawled out on my bed reading it in my quiet room," she said. "I don't remember if my mom told me that she and the author had been incarcerated in the same camps, Tanforan and Topaz." Lee-Tai's grandparents, Matsusaburo George Hibi and Hisako Shimizu Hibi, were established artists. They made art in camp and taught at the Topaz Art School, founded by their friend, the painter Chiura Obata. Matsusaburo wrote a brief history of the school.[112] "Training in art maintains high ideals among our people," he wrote, "for its object is to prevent their minds from remaining on the plains, to encourage human spirits to dwell high above the mountains."

Years later, Lee-Tai revisited the Topaz Art School in her children's book, *A Place Where Sunflowers Grow*, which tells the story of Mari, a young girl whose sadness and confusion about her and her family's situation are lifted and

---

112. "History and Development of Topaz Art School," which is now in the Smithsonian Archives of American Art.

alleviated by making art. "It was as if, with every drawing she created, Mari found another question to ask and the courage to ask it," Lee-Tai writes in the book.

"Before writing the story," said Lee-Tai, "I wrote the introduction, which gives some history of the incarceration and my family's experience. I remember sitting at my desktop and crying as I wrote it, just feeling the anger flow out of me, anger for what my family and others in their community had endured."

Meri Mitsuyoshi learned about incarceration when she was ten. Her parents had *Executive Order 9066*. Her mother gave her *Journey to Topaz* and inscribed it: *Daddy and Mommy made a journey to Topaz too*. One night, her family watched a documentary on PBS about incarceration. "I recall blurting out that I felt lucky I didn't have to endure what my parents did. They smiled quietly. There were no more words."

When Kelly Toppenberg was in fifth or sixth grade, she read *Farewell to Manzanar*. "Beyond that, I don't think anyone in my family talked about it or explained it in a way that I understood."

"I also read *Farewell to Manzanar* as a fifth grader," Mia Ayumi Malhotra continued, "and had some vague sense that it was important."

"The summer before I started middle school," said Yoshino Jasso, "my Mom took me to Kinokuniya in Little Tokyo and told me to pick out some books. I ended up getting *Kira Kira* and *Weedflower* by Cynthia Kadohata, which filled in some blanks for me.

"I grew up reading Cynthia Kadohata," said Kai Sase Ebens. "I was particularly fascinated by *Weedflower*. The book details many aspects of camp life, from the preservation of cultural tradition to the scorpions. I would only later connect the dots to my own ancestry."

When Mark Kuroda was in middle school, he read *Journey to Topaz*. He asked his family if they had gone through what Uchida describes. "There was a sense for the first time in my life that they didn't want to talk about it. My father was born there and has spoken of it but almost from a third person point of view."

In Lori Watanabe's middle school US history textbook, Pearl Harbor was featured prominently, with a full-page photo and several paragraphs of text, but Watanabe could not find a single word about incarceration. When she mustered the courage to confront her white teacher about it, he responded, blankly, that he knew *nothing* about it.

"I am in sixth grade now," said Rhys Nelsen, "and I have not learned anything about incarceration."

When Renee Tajima-Peña was in sixth grade, she gave an oral report on incarceration. She interviewed her mother and grandmother, who were in Heart Mountain. "When I was giving my report," she said, "my teacher, Mrs. Counts, screamed that I was lying, my mom and grandma fabricated the story and it could never happen in America. That's when I understood the full weight of the injustice. I was super pissed off. It was the year I read *The Autobiography of Malcolm X* and led my first school walkout. Probably why I'm a filmmaker today."

After a field trip to the Museum of Tolerance (Los Angeles) in sixth grade, Taylor Ingman's class talked about communities that had faced mass detention or death based solely on their race. Japanese Americans were not included. "When I brought it up, my teacher shot me down. I don't remember exactly what she said, but I clearly felt she was trying to convey something along the lines of *we aren't talking about that right now*. This was the first time I felt embarrassed or ashamed of talking about it."

Autumn Yamamoto learned about incarceration in sixth grade. "The teacher took the time to make derisive comments about my last name," she said. "She was discussing the attack on Pearl Harbor, noted that I shared the same name as Admiral Yamamoto [commander-in-chief of the Japanese Imperial Army], made a flippant comment that a Yamamoto was behind killing many American soldiers but that they *got us back* by dropping bombs on Hiroshima and Nagasaki."

When Kathryn Nishibayashi was in seventh grade, her grandmother gave her a stack of books about incarceration, including *Citizen 13660* and *Farewell to Manzanar*. "I vaguely remember my grandma giving me the books as sort of a silent signal she was done talking about it."

There was one paragraph about incarceration in Erin Shigaki's seventh grade Washington State history book. "I knew there had to be more," she said. "My mom suggested that I ask my grandmothers if I could interview them, and they both acquiesced. I gave an oral report to the class full of dry facts. I remember I felt self-righteous. Our teacher, Mrs. Hogan, who was white, quietly wept in the back corner."

"My first remembrance of *knowing* comes from history class in middle school," said Starr Miyata. "When incarceration was mentioned, I had a visceral physical reaction of sadness to the point of feeling sick, and a sense of knowing that this was something that happened to my family. I had a similar reaction when the bombing of Hiroshima was mentioned."

When Lisa Nori Nishimura Pawin was in middle school, she noticed that her US History book had "a measly 1.75 paragraphs about incarceration. I raised my hand to eagerly add more information. My teacher was thrilled and pulled me aside after class to ask me to make a presentation. This would occur several more times. My classmates would tease me and call me *Internment Girl*."

Learning about WWII in middle school, Natalia Arai mentioned to her class that her family had been incarcerated. After school, a group of girls confronted her on the basketball court. One of them called Arai a *Jap bitch*. "I gave her a black eye and got suspended," Arai said. When her father came to pick her up, she was afraid he would be upset. "He said he was proud of me. He bought me a rainbow icy."

Years earlier, when Arai's father returned to school from Minidoka, the teacher asked everyone to share what they had done over the summer. When Arai's father talked about camp, the teacher said he was lying and sent him to the principal's office.

When Dana Kyoko Sato was in middle school, her teacher introduced the unit on WWII by saying that they were going to focus on what was happening in the United States, but did not mention Japanese American incarceration. When Sato insisted they cover it, the teacher asked her to "put something together."

When Elizabeth Fugikawa was in seventh grade, her social studies teacher asked her to give a presentation on incarceration. "I was on the verge of tears, both from sorrow and anger over how many innocent people were imprisoned and hurt. My teacher was engaged, but I remember feeling like no one else in the class really cared. I felt pretty defeated."

When Emily Hanako Momohara was in middle school, she was given the assignment of drawing the floor plan of a building. She drew her grandmother's barrack in Minidoka. Her grandmother helped. "That is probably the most information I received directly from a family member," she said.

When Liana Hisako Tai was in seventh grade, she made a model of the Topaz Art School, based on a scene in *A Place Where Sunflowers Grow*, a children's book written by her mother, Amy Lee-Tai, which was based, in turn, on the experience of Lee-Tai's grandparents, Matsusaburo and

Hisako, and her mother, Ibuki Hibi Lee. Tai made a classroom out of a cigar box, paper for the roof, cardboard furniture, polymer clay for the students and teacher. "I would feel extremely excited," Tai said, about when camp came up in class, "and, at the same time, a dread would rush over me, my heart would start beating out of my chest and my face would turn red. Suddenly, my class of almost all white students would turn slowly to look at me like I was a statue in a museum."

When Karla Hora Powell was in seventh grade, she interviewed her parents. "I remember Dad saying that when they arrived at Poston, the barracks were still being built. He and his brothers were able to make a few dollars helping with the construction." Her mother described riding in Jeeps with soldiers. "I remember her saying the girls did not go anywhere by themselves, day or night, as some girls were assaulted and some were raped by other internees. When I gave my report, the class was very quiet."

In seventh or eighth grade Social Studies, Lauren Yamasaki-Cramer read *The Diary of Anne Frank*. "I raised my hand and told the teacher that my father had been in a concentration camp. She asked if my father would be willing to speak to the class. That was the first time I heard more details around what he and his family experienced. My classmates applauded and a few even came up to me to mention how cool it was that my dad came to class. I felt like a celebrity."

When she was in eighth grade, Yoshino Jasso made a model of a horse stall in Tanforan, where her great-grandmother was incarcerated, out of popsicle sticks and "tiny foil can lids, to keep scorpions from crawling in and out of holes in the walls." She got a C+. "The project was supposed to be about genocide," Jasso said, "but the incarceration was not murder-y enough."

Should the Japanese have been interned? Leigh Ann Tomooka's ninth grade English teacher asked. Her class was reading *Farewell to Manzanar*. "I never thought it was debatable," said Tomooka. "The US had already given us reparations. However, students in my class echoed the words of their parents who defended the decision, and so did my teacher."

"In high school," Miko Charbonneau continued, "we read *The Greatest Generation*, which mentions the reparation checks. One of my best friends said to me, *Well see, it wasn't that bad, they got paid a lot of money.*"

When Lisa Hernandez was in high school, she wrote a paper analyzing the case for reparations. "I remember the teacher saying she never heard about it." The class was called *Civil Liberties*.

"I first understood the camps as symbolic and dark during the violent nationalism following 9/11," said Sean Miura. "A couple weeks after 9/11, I had this unusually clear dream in which a close high school friend, a practicing Muslim, was sent to a camp. This was after that friend told me she was scared of being sent to a camp. This was around the time when a student came up to her in the hallway and told her to stop flying planes into 'our' buildings. This was before she signed up to do the morning announcements and, with a defiant smile, wished everyone a happy Ramadan."

When Kay Yatabe was in high school, she watched the "Nisei" episode of Walter Cronkite's *The Twentieth Century*. It was "my first clear memory of my parent's incarceration," she said. Her mother always said that she had a "great time in camp," but Yatabe noticed, while watching the show, that her mother had tears in her eyes.

When Kathy Shie Nuss was in high school, her mother began collecting books on incarceration, including Michi Weglyn's *Years of Infamy* and Allan Bosworth and Roger Baldwin's *America's Concentration Camps*. The first book

Nuss read on the subject was *City in the Sun*, a novel about Poston, and the first novel about incarceration to be published. It was written by Karen Kehoe, a white woman, who worked for the chief of internal security in Gila River and later for the education department. Nuss remembers especially a story in the book about a riot. "I was shocked and asked my Dad about it," Nuss said. "He was very nonchalant about it, said *Yeah I was there.*"

When Debbi Michiko Florence was in high school, she interviewed her father, who was in Crystal City. "It was the first time I learned my father and his family had been incarcerated. I asked my dad, *What was the scariest thing that happened to you?* He responded that it was when he was playing with a flashlight at night outdoors and suddenly all the guard tower spotlights shined on him."

When Christina Hiromi Hobbs was in ninth grade, she interviewed her grandmother for a social studies paper. "It felt very powerful to me that I was a freshman at the same age she was incarcerated at Minidoka," Hobbs said. "It made her descriptions of the camp feel alive. She was initially incarcerated at the Portland Assembly Center, and the image and sounds of a slaughterhouse have always stayed in my mind."[113]

When Kimiko Guthrie was in high school, she wrote a story about a young girl, Fumi, whose parents, preparing for removal, are forced to sell the family hotel to a white man. Fearing that he might take her new bicycle too, she hides it in a blackberry bush. The story ends with Fumi and her family's first night in Santa Anita. The final sentence: "She lay awake for what seemed like hours, until at last she fell asleep, despite the cold, the rank smell of manure, and the emptiness in her stomach and heart."

---

113. "All through the day she could hear the animals being killed," Hobbs wrote, in her paper (Gunn High School, Period C, 2009).

Kimiko's mother, her mother's siblings, and their parents, were in Santa Anita and Rohwer. "I had never written a whole story before," Guthrie said. "I remember it pouring out of me. I felt as though my family members, but especially my grandfather, were speaking to me through it."[114]

When Brittany Arita was in tenth grade, she did a project on incarceration for her *Jazz Age to the Holocaust* class. She interviewed her mother, who talked about her father-in-law's experience in the horse stalls in Santa Anita, his father scrubbing the walls to get rid of the stench. She made a video using her grandparents' photos. It ended with Fort Minor's "Kenji," a song by Mike Shinoda, whose family was also in Santa Anita. It was "the first time I had ever seen a reference to the camps in pop culture," Arita said.

There was one paragraph about incarceration in Patrick Shiroishi's high school history textbook. "I went to ask my grandma about it, and she shut down and wouldn't talk to me."

When Hana Maruyama was in tenth grade, she interviewed her great-uncle and grandmother. "My great-uncle was very open to answering questions, but my grandma was not," she said. "She ended up shutting down about two questions in. I think I asked my grandmother something like, *What do you think of FDR?* and she just said, *I hate him. I hate him.*

For a debate in her eleventh grade US Government class, Autumn Yamamoto had to argue *for* incarceration. "They wanted to *challenge* me, knowing that I was Japanese American," she said. Afterwards, her teacher was "semi-apologetic about it."

---

114. Years later, Guthrie revisited the scene in her novel, *Block Seventeen*. In one of several flashbacks, a young girl lies on her cot in a horse stall, unable to sleep, listening to "all the strange noises of the stadium forming a disturbing symphony."

When Chelsey Oda was in eleventh grade, she wrote a paper on incarceration for history class, which she read out loud. "I got a little choked up," she said, "and kids in my class couldn't figure out why. They just thought I was being dramatic or weird."

When she was in high school, Suzanne Kimiko Onodera—whose father Koji designed the cover for the 1976 edition of John Okada's *No-No Boy*—tried talking to her classmates about incarceration, but most of them did not believe her "and thought I made it up to get attention."

"Oh the internment camps," said Rea Tajiri's high school teacher, "everyone makes a big deal out it, but they were nothing. It was like a vacation for Japanese Americans—isn't that right Rea?"

"No," Tajiri responded. "I don't think so..."

When Allison Takeuchi was a senior in high school, she took part in a reenactment of the forced removal. Saturday, late April, Watsonville, CA. She was invited by Mas Hashimoto, a retired high school history teacher, who was incarcerated in Poston. For her part, Takeuchi, whose grandparents were also in Poston, walked down Main Street carrying a suitcase, then sat behind a barbed wire fence, as people on the other side stared at her. "My family had always been pretty open and vocal about their experiences," Takeuchi told me. "There was never a sense of shame or even anger, but a matter-of-factness about it. And yet, going through the reenactment brought me a deep sense of sadness."

It took eighteen months to plan the reenactment, many more than it took to build the camps. The youngest reenactor was two, the oldest ninety-eight. "I instructed them never to smile," Hashimoto told me, "especially if a photographer or reporter asked."[115]

"Between remembrance and re-enactment: there is waiting," writes Jackie Wang, in her poem, "Waiting for Godel."[116] It began with the Star-Spangled Banner, then Sandy Lydon, local historian: "We're going to do a little time travel," he said, standing in front of the Veterans Memorial Building. At the top of the steps, a white woman and man sat at a table. Three Japanese American women appeared, each carrying a suitcase. They walked up the steps, women and children lined up behind them. A family sat on suitcases beside an Army jeep. They waited for the buses (1942 Greyhound), for something both more and less tangible—pivotal, climactic—to happen. There was an air of uncertainty, not only in waiting to be taken to an unknown destination, but in reenacting the experience of the survivors, some of whom were in the audience. The buses drove to a theater down the street, cyclone fences in the lobby, paintings of guard towers—by Howard Ikemoto, who was a child in Tule Lake—flanking the stage.

Judy Doering-Nielsen, former mayor of Watsonville, dismissed the reenactment, saying, "It doesn't solve anything. It doesn't do anything other than to bring back old memories." She was also the president of the local historical association, which, according to their website, is devoted to "keeping the stories of yesteryear [aka *old memories*] alive for future generations."

"I believe that generational trauma is a real thing," said Takeuchi. "Whether it is passed on in our marrow or through the way we talk about past trauma. It's like a scar

---

115. Hashimoto passed away shortly after we corresponded. His local paper, *The Pajaronian*, reported that the last thing he did the night before he died was watch *Flower Drum Song* with his wife.
116. Jackie Wang, "Waiting for Godel," *The Sunflower Cast a Spell to Save Us From the Void* (Brooklyn, NY: Nightboat Books, 2021)

on your back that you got a long time ago. You never really notice or pay attention to it, but every once in a while someone will point it out or you'll catch a glimpse of it in the mirror."

"They called us evacuees," said Joni Kimoto. Tuesday morning, first period, Beaumont Middle School, Portland (December 2016). Forty students, mostly white, sat in tiny chairs in the library. Five Black students sat in the back. A girl in a hijab crossed her arms over her lap and buried her head. A Betsy Ross flag, thirteen stars in a circle, hung on the wall. The students—with the look of children being made to sit before a person who is presented as a living example of what is often mistaken for ancient material—had been reading *Hotel on the Corner of Bitter and Sweet*, a novel by Jamie Ford about two friends, a Chinese American boy and a Japanese American girl who are separated when the girl is sent to Minidoka, where Kimoto was incarcerated as a child.

She began by telling a story about the morning in 1942 when the FBI showed up at her door and asked if there were guns in the house. "Yes," she said. She was three. Her parents were mortified. The FBI asked where. She led them to the attic. Inside an old chest was a toy gun. Kimoto's parents and the FBI laughed. Their laughter had nothing in common.

Kimoto and her family were forced from their home and taken by bus to the northern edge of Portland. On Sundays, traffic slowed to a crawl along North Swift so that white people could stare through the fence. Kimoto and her family were detained for four months. Then taken by train six hundred miles east. "There was a dust storm when we got off the train and my mom grabbed my hand. I remember her saying to me—Joni, this is our new home—and crying."

These words are printed on an interpretive sign in Minidoka that overlooks one of the original barracks.

They lived in Block 32, Barrack 7. Kimoto was very sociable, visited everyone, always came away with handfuls of candy, so much that her father made her wear a sign around her neck that said DO NOT FEED ME. She also wore a tiny ornamental slipper her aunt knitted. She showed it to the students. It slipped out of her hand and fell to the carpet. She held up a wooden cane her grandfather carved. The students passed it around.[117]

Sitting there in the middle school library, I thought of all of the classrooms throughout the United States where Japanese American students have been made to discover how insignificant incarceration is to the study of history. I thought of how many times teachers have put the responsibility of educating those classrooms—of *teaching*—on those Japanese American students. I thought of how the teachers disguised their laziness and exploitation of those students as an opportunity *for the student*. In those classrooms, the story of Japanese American incarceration, whether presented as a largely immaterial footnote to the death camps in Europe, as a dark but ultimately endurable chapter in American history, or not presented at all, was made to be *about* the Japanese American student in the room, if there was one, the effect of which was to amplify their singularity, isolation and shame, and to force upon them the authority of history.

---

117. In Aisuke Kondo's video, *here where you stood*, he takes his great-grandfather's wooden cane to Topaz, walks with it into the desert, swings it, beats the air with it. When he strikes it against the ground, it breaks in half. "I did not mean to," he told me.

JAPANESE AMERICAN INCARCERATION FOR CHILDREN

I DISCOVERED SOMETHING ABOUT YUMI'S RELATION-ship to books: if I cry the first time we read a book together, it is very likely that she will not want to read the book again. This has happened several times, most often with books, written for children, about Japanese American incarceration.

Yumi has seen me cry more times in the past year than I have seen my parents cry in four decades. She is, when I cry, very comforting. She asks what is wrong or tries to be funny. But not when we are reading together. If I cry while reading a book with her, she becomes tense, sometimes scared, most often frustrated or annoyed. Then it feels like I have ruined the book and have taken from her the experience of developing, in her own way, a relationship with the story, which is, in part, an emotional relationship, therefore a relationship with her emotions. But sometimes my emotions take over, overwhelm the story and Yumi's experience of it, and I cry, I cannot help it.

The protagonists of children's books about Japanese American incarceration are, for the most part, children. A cat, a man who is lost, children. The subject is the children's experience, which, prior to an awareness of the conditions of their citizenship, is that of developing a relationship to being bewildered, to bewilderment, which manifests as a sadness the children are unable to name. The reader—assuming they are an adult, ushering a child through the story—understands, or might understand, at least superficially, what the barbed wire and guard towers mean, which puts the children in the position of having to catch up to the reader. The subject of children's books about Japanese American incarceration is, then, the children's coming into an awareness of being—and being the last to know that they are—enemies of their country, which means being forced into an antagonistic relationship with themselves. Sadness is one way of portraying it. The children, helped by family members and friends, occasionally and most ridiculously by white friends and neighbors, but most often and most mournfully by themselves, discover and invent ways of transforming their sadness into a bittersweet understanding that life is much longer than any individual trauma, even as trauma is much longer not only than life, but of lives, generations.

I cried the first time Yumi and I read *Fish For Jimmy*, written and illustrated by Katie Yamasaki (2013). Jimmy, incarcerated in a "dusty internment camp" in a "desolate land," loses his appetite. His mother and his brother Taro urge him to eat, but he refuses. He stops playing with other children, begins to lose his memory of life before camp. One night, Taro cuts a hole in the fence and runs to a mountain. "A trickle of water led to a quiet pool, where still, black water, reflected the night sky." He slips his hands into the water and pulls up seven fish, bright orange and yellow. The next morning, Taro gives the fish to Jimmy, who eats them, and comes back to life.

On the final page, Taro and his father—who has rejoined the family after being incarcerated in a DOJ prison—stare through the barbed wire fence at the reader. When I reached their faces and the final sentence—"Taro showed

Father how, each week, he would creep beyond the fence to the free air of the mountains to find fish for Jimmy"—I gasped, then started crying. Yumi, silent throughout, looked at me with a grave expression, pushed the book closed with her hand, and said "No."

In *A Place Where Sunflowers Grow*, written by Amy Lee-Tai and illustrated by Felicia Hoshino (2006), Mari is walking with her father in Topaz. "Mama and I are worried about you," Mari's father says. "We know things are tough here, but you barely talk or laugh anymore." Mari does not say anything. They keep walking in silence, "beneath watchtowers where military police pointed guns at anyone they feared might escape."

How is Mari expected to talk or laugh with guns pointed at her? The book is about art, its redeeming encouragement. Mari takes an art class. The fact that there were art classes suggests how long incarceration lasted: long enough for a civilization to rise from the dust and produce art education. Mari watches the other students fill their paper with colorful drawings, but her paper is blank. She is sorrowful, in a malaise. When her teacher encourages her to draw something from her life before camp, she comes back to life. Mari draws her house and backyard in California, sunflowers touching the sky. The past achieves the horizon of the future.

In *Flowers from Mariko*, written by Rick Noguchi and Deneen Jenks and illustrated by Michelle Kumata (2001), young readers are introduced to the trailer parks where families resettled after camp. Resettlement is embodied by a father's struggle to find work and his daughter's attempt to take hold of that struggle and lessen it. Mariko's father scavenges tools from dumpsters. He finds two packets of seeds and gives them to Mariko. She plants the seeds in the dirt outside their trailer. It takes time for them to bloom, but Mariko is committed, and the day they bloom, her father finds work. It is Mariko's commitment, fortitude, and belief, that bring life to the bleakness. They celebrate.

Mariko and her father dance, Mariko with a flower in her hair, her father with a flower tucked into his shirt. "Everything was going to be fine, Mariko decided."

Mariko, Mari, and Taro have all been drawn into the work of making things better. Their parents are not absent, but are not afforded the agency or the ability to bring their children's stories to a place in which they might feel that everything is going to be fine. Feeling fine is a decision reached by the children, through the persistence of their efforts, and the endurance of their memories. The parents are guides, part ghost. Their struggles are only as explicit as the impact they have on their children, who, through melancholia, are watching.

"Emi didn't want her big sister to see her cry," is the first sentence of *The Bracelet*, written by Yoshiko Uchida and illustrated by Joanna Yardley (1976). Emi and her family are being forced from their home. It is their last day. The doorbell rings. Emi opens the door to find not military police, but her best friend, a white girl named Laurie Madison, on the porch, holding a small box. A gift—a bracelet. Emi swears never to take it off, but shortly after arriving at Tanforan, it goes missing. Emi fears that without the bracelet she will forget Laurie, therefore life before camp. As if it was Laurie who was left behind. The last sentence of the book: "Emi knew she would never forget Laurie, ever."

The menace of the dangling *ever*. The book concludes with the white friend as the means of daily endurance. Laurie Madison is not the only white friend, but is a recurring character. In Ann Malaspina's *A Scarf for Keiko* (2019), the white friend is Sam, who knits Keiko a scarf, which she wears in camp. In Cynthia Grady's *Write To Me* (2017), the white friend is a librarian, Miss Breed—based on Clara Breed, librarian at the San Diego Public Library— who sends books to the children in camp. The children are dependent upon their white friends for release, however momentary, from the reality of their incarceration, and to stay connected to the world beyond the barbed wire. The white friends appear at the beginning of the stories to say goodbye, become the stewards of Japanese American memory, then project themselves into a future that they, through their gift-giving, make possible, and where they are magnanimously waiting.

When the children arrived in camp, the schools had no books, and there were no schools. I learned this in a poem by Heather Nagami, "Acts of Translation," which was the first poem I read about Japanese American incarceration written by a descendant. I was in graduate school, just becoming aware of poetry written by survivors, which made Nagami's poem and her book *Hostile* feel like rallying cries from the future. In the poem, Nagami returns to Poston, where her grandparents were incarcerated and where her mother was born, and attempts to make sense of their experience and her relation to it. Her mother's birth is announced in the first line: "'I was born in a hospital,' she tells me, proudly (Figure 10.57), 'driven out of the camp to a hospital' (Figure 10.57)." Figure 10.57 corresponds to an image in *Confinement and Ethnicity*, an archeological study of the incarceration sites: a photograph of one of the camp's hospitals, which, as Nagami describes it, "Looks more like a house…Wooden porch with railings and wood slats sliding off. Garden hose hanging off side of wall. Looks more like an old house in the South…Screen door tilted, hanging on by a hinge. Chevy parked crooked out back."[118]

118. Jeffrey F. Burton, Mary M. Farrell, Florence B. Lord, Richard W. Lord, *Confinement and Ethnicity: An Overview of World War II Japanese American Relocation Sites*. (Tucson, AZ: Western Archeological and Conservation Center)

I saw Nagami read "Acts of Translation" on the 75th anniversary of Executive Order 9066, at the Tucson Desert Art Museum. The museum used to be a mall. The galleries were stores. The event was arranged as if for a wedding, rows of white folding chairs divided by an aisle. In the next room, an 8mm film of Poston's construction was being projected on the wall. White men in white shirts and overalls poured concrete, unloaded bed frames from a truck. It was silent but emitted an obsequious energy. Nagami stood in the aisle and read slowly:

> Since no arrangements had been made, evacuees built
>   their own classrooms.
> "But mom didn't know if there was going to be one
>   where we were going."
> West of Blocks 19 and 30.
> "So, she brought…

Her voice cracked. She read the line again, "So, she brought…" but her voice cracked again. She stared into her poem like she was searching for herself in a mirror. "So, she brought…" her voice cracking a third time. Poston was being built—pluckily, grotesquely—on the other side of the wall. A crew of 5,000 men worked from March into May 1942, when they were joined by 260 Japanese American volunteers, and yet "no arrangements had been made" for schools, so it was left to mothers to bring—which means also to invent—*everything*. I say Nagami's voice cracked, but she cried. Her mother was sitting in the front row. I tried to imagine what it might have felt like for her to listen to her daughter recite and have difficulty reciting a poem about the place where she was born a prisoner. It felt like the memorial and everything we were meant to understand was distilled into how Nagami's mother might have been feeling and into Nagami crying through her mother's words then recomposing herself to go on. "So, she brought... encyclopedias... for us and for the other children."

Children's books about Japanese American incarceration are burdened with the obligation of also being history books. The history has experienced a strained, frustrated life. The more it is told, the less the public seems to remember, so when it is told—most frequently provoked, these days, by present injustice—it begins with a reiteration of the facts. It is less about facts though, and more about having to start, with each telling, all over again, to appease a citizenry that is not listening, that is defined by its refusal to listen.

The repetition of violence into themes, themes into oblivion, begins to sound like a song. Is that how Yumi hears *December 7, 1941, Pearl Harbor, FBI, barracks, barbed wire, guard towers, guns*? The sounds precede meaning, and I imagine the meaning forms out of the sounds, their repetition, and out of the illustrations accompanying the sounds, the repetition mimicking the effort to combat willed forgetting and mimicking the way trauma converts facts into affirmations; and I imagine that the realization of meaning will come, if it comes, when the sounds are repeated outside of the books, in life, where the sounds are unexpected and where they will seem even more naked, cruel, and disarming, but what is it that makes us remember?

I did not grow up with children's books about or that mentioned Japanese American incarceration. There were not many. Yumi has *The Bracelet*, Marlene Shigekawa's *Blue Jay in the Desert* (1993), Ken Mochizuki's *Baseball Saved Us* (1993), Eve Bunting's *So Far from the Sea* (1998), *Flowers From Mariko*, Allen Say's *Home of the Brave* (2002) and *Music for Alice* (2004), *A Place Where Sunflowers Grow*, *Fish For Jimmy*, Loriene Honda's *The Cat Who Chose to Dream* (2014), *Write To Me*, *A Scarf for Keiko*, Kyo Maclear's *It Began With a Page: How Gyo Fujikawa Drew the Way* (2019), and Maggie Tokuda-Hall's *Love in the Library* (2022). In *Home of the Brave*, written and illustrated by Allen Say, a man goes kayaking down a river and ends up in camp. He sees two children and offers to help them find their way home. They walk through a dust storm and arrive into rows of barracks set against a ghostlike mountain. "A group of children stood before him," dozens of children, all the way to the mountain. "Then all at once the small mouths opened." The children cry out for the man to take them home. Then "two beams of light slashed at the children." Guard towers, in which the guards are invisible. The children, illuminated by the excoriating lights, run, but in the illustration, only the man is differentiated. Even more haunting is the illustration, and the description, of the children as "one large body with many eyes." They stare directly at the reader, eyebrows arched, mouths open, in a way that looks like they are apparitions, chanting, tongues about to turn into snakes.

The children the man first encounters are based on Hiroko and Miyuki Mochida, sisters, and two of the subjects of a photograph taken by Dorothea Lange, May 8, 1942. The Mochidas—nine family members, each wearing an ID tag, four duffel bags between them—are waiting for the bus to take them from Hayward, California, to Tanforan. Hiroko and Miyuki's expressions come closest to evoking the kind of sadness that might satisfy the mind of someone who would like to reduce the experience of dispossession to that seemingly accessible condition, which is probably why the sisters' image has been reproduced so many times, except that they look like they are wondering why there is a woman taking their picture. In *Home of the Brave*, they look weather-beaten, abandoned. "It occurred to me to lift the two girls out of the photograph and introduce them into the book," Say said in an interview.

He was inspired to write *Home of the Brave* after seeing an exhibition about Manzanar at JANM. He had already written the pages where the man goes kayaking down the river and had intended to put the man through a much different journey, but after seeing the exhibition, decided to send him to camp. On the final page, the man throws a handful of ID tags into the air and, surrounded by children, watches as they fly over the mountains.

"They went home," says a child.

"Yes, they went home," says the man.

Hiroko and Miyuki are also on the cover of Susan Kamei's *When Can We Go Back to America?* (2021). It is not a children's book, but a 700-page history book. Lange's photograph is wrapped around the cover, Miyuki on the front, Hiroko on the spine, barbed wire across their bodies. Also, Miyuki is cut off below her eyes. Hiroko and Miyuki did not, on May 8, 1942, know where they were going. The camps did not yet exist because they had not yet been built. Hiroko and Miyuki are, as they are in *Home of the Brave*, rushed into incarceration and preserved there.

On December 7, 2021, the 80th anniversary of Pearl Harbor, I moderated a conversation between Kamei and George Takei about their books on Japanese American incarceration. Takei's memoir, *They Called Us Enemy* (2019), is a graphic novel about his experience in camp. He was five when he and his family were incarcerated in Santa Anita, then Rohwer. During the conversation, Takei told a story about a conversation he had with his father years after the war, a conversation that, he said, still haunted him.

He and his father were at the dinner table talking, as they had many times before, about incarceration. "Daddy," Takei said—reenacting the conversation—"why did you go? It was wrong. You should have spoken up, stood up…Daddy, you led us like sheep to slaughter." Takei's father was silent. After what felt to Takei like an eternity, his father said, "Well, maybe you're right." Then he got up from the table, went to his room and closed the door. Takei felt ashamed, wanted desperately to apologize. He wanted to knock on his father's door. But he did not. He went to bed, thinking he would apologize in the morning. But he did not. "I never apologized," Takei told us, near tears. "And now I can't."

I cry when stories end. I cry *that* stories end. It is beautiful to see Mariko dancing and Mari drawing and Jimmy eating, but it is heartbreaking to know that the children are only at the beginning of their sentence and that the burden of releasing themselves from it is theirs and will continue to be, even as the inheritance of that burden and the complexity of what it means to be released, will pass from them to their children and grandchildren. I cry because the need to tell these stories as stories *that end* is a desire, in part, to pay tribute to these children, now elders, now passed, and the stories they told and the wound that extended from their childhood into the future and into the need to tell stories, even—especially—if the stories sought relief from the pain of the wound, by telling stories in order to end them.

Japanese Americans who were born or who were very young in the detention centers and concentration camps are now in their late seventies and early eighties. They are the final generation of camp survivors, the final generation who can speak directly from the experience. And yet they are also, because they were newborn, one, two, three years old, the generation of survivors least likely to remember. The survivors who remember most vividly and who are able to share what they remember, were still children, so their memories, filtered through their perspective as adults, now as elders, are the memories of children. We have entered the phase of historical remembrance that is reliant almost entirely upon the experiences and the memories of children.

The first incarceration site that Yumi visited was the Tucson Federal Prison Camp, on Mount Lemmon, north of Tucson. It was rebranded the Gordon Hirabayashi Recreation Site because it was where Hirabayashi was incarcerated for refusing the curfew, exclusion order, and to register for removal. It is an easy drive up Catalina Highway—which was built by the prisoners—to mile marker 7 and left onto Prison Camp Road. It is now a campground. Where the prisoners slept are campsites. The foundation of the administration building is broken but still visible. Yumi learned to walk in that desert, hike in that desert, identify cactus and trees in that desert. She collected acorns and seeds, "treasures," she called them. Crickets jumped out of the grass. The madrone, with its iridescent crimson bark, looked like mummified flames. I noticed, from the hills, that the voices of people below—having picnics, setting up trailers, tents—were perfectly clear, which made me realize that the administrators were listening and could hear every word.

Lisa told me that when I read children's books about Japanese American incarceration with Yumi, my voice changes, lowers, goes flat. The books are meant to be full of hope and redemption, children needing only to turn the world in their hands, and redeem, with the boundlessness of their youth and the light of their inextinguishable minds, the darkness passing through it.

Are all children's books about Japanese American incarceration—are all children's books in general—manuals preparing children for the moment in their lives, and for the time after, when they will be left behind and/or abandoned?

Last night, Yumi saw *Fish For Jimmy* leaning against the wall behind my desk and picked it up. "Let's read this!" she said. It seemed to be going okay at first. Maybe enough time had passed. She was silent, listening—through the barbed wire and guard towers, the guards and their guns, through

Jimmy refusing to eat, becoming depressed, through Taro escaping camp, pulling fish out of the water. But when things began improving for Jimmy, Yumi let out a long sigh, said, "This story is too hard." Then she turned away from the book, rolled off the bed and ran out of the room.

DRY BED OF THE RIVER
OF SOULS

AFTER THEIR FIRST WINTER IN PRISON, AND AFTER THE
snow melted, the Issei at Fort Missoula noticed, all over the
prison grounds, stones. Stones of infinite color, shape and
design. "Perhaps this is the site of an ancient river or sea,"
wrote Iwao Matsushita, one of the prisoners, in a letter to
his wife, Hanaye, "for polished pebbles are strewn all over
and everyone is immersed in collecting these stones," adding: "like children" (March 9, 1942).[119]

Hanaye received Iwao's letter at home in Seattle. She
would soon be removed to Puyallup, then Minidoka. Iwao
was detained by the FBI in the hours after Pearl Harbor.
He arrived in Missoula on December 28, 1941. The valley
that Sunday was covered in snow. In the spring, the ground
softened, stones grew like flowers. The men gathered and
polished the stones, made jewelry, sculptures, gifts for their
families. Iwao mailed stones to Hanaye. "So avid is this
stone picking," he wrote, "that it is said that anyone not
involved in this hobby is not human."

---

119. Iwao Matsushita, *Imprisoned Apart: The World War II Correspondence
of an Issei Couple*, ed. Louis Fiset (Seattle: University of Washington
Press, 1997)

Gathering stones was a way to be, in the midst of being criminalized by the country to which they had committed their futures, "human, like children." But children did not need to be a likeness, the innocence of the men, or the emphasis of their condition. They were there too—in the camps, stone-picking their own prison grounds. "We were children, hunting stones," writes David Mura, in his poem "An Argument: On 1942."[120]

I moved to Missoula in August 2004 to begin my first semester in the MFA program in Creative Writing at the University of Montana. The commitment to be, or becoming, a poet was less about enrolling in a graduate program, and more about being close to my grandfather.

I felt his presence, especially at night. Some nights I heard his voice. Distant, the amplitude of an ember. I wanted to bring his presence and his voice to where I was, or bring myself down to where I felt him to be: buried—beneath the accumulation of withholdings and refusals by which the truth of his experience was obscured. By buried I mean also arrested: that some part of him had not managed, or been permitted, to be released, to join the rest of himself in the future.

I spent four years wandering Fort Missoula. I did not know what I was looking for. I felt like the woman in Brynn Saito's poem, "Stone Returns, 70 Years Later," who, visiting Manzanar, "paces the length / of the barrack blocks, // the dead weight of midnight like a sea." She drops a stone into her pocket, "slips into the night to stand in the field // and summon ghosts." The woman caresses the stone like a rosary. What, if and when the ghosts come, will happen? What will she—what will I—do? Stop pacing? Go home?

---

120. David Mura, "An Argument: On 1942," *After We Lost Our Way* (New York: E.P. Dutton, 1989)

I brought with me *Imprisoned Apart: The World War II Correspondence of an Issei Couple*, a collection of Iwao and Hanaye Matsushita's letters. My grandparents, who met shortly before my grandfather was sent to Fort Missoula, did not write letters to each other, none my grandmother saved or could remember. Iwao and Hanaye's letters became surrogates, idealizations. They wrote beauty and sadness, about when they would see each other again. I was drawn especially to their inventories of the weather, wildlife and wildflowers:

"Frozen fog makes branches beautiful with snow flowers against the azure sky...Spring is deep, but the weather is unsettled...Garden flowers are blooming one by one, but we have seldom chance to see them...I've enjoyed the dry pressed flowers enclosed in the last letter and cried with nostalgia remembering the fun days we've had...Listening to the quiet rush of the river in the morning, I feel as though you are calling to me. Even the coyote's howl is nostalgic...I haven't heard any coyotes recently, though once in a while I see a scorpion...The spring flowers don't move me as much since I saw them all last year...Almost a year has wasted away since we parted...I plan on turning to ashes."

I read the letters in the barracks, the long fields, the road, by the river. I had a hard time believing the barracks, so undemonstrative, with their charming, willowy air, corresponded to my grandfather's prison. Iwao's letters were written not far from my grandfather. If I could hear Iwao's pen moving across the paper, then I might be able to hear the sounds that surrounded his pen, his breathing, the sounds in the room, that surrounded the room, out the door, my grandfather somewhere on the edge of those sounds.

I was not introduced to the work of a single Japanese American poet in graduate school. Nor, for that matter, in any classroom between preschool and Missoula, Montana.

There were no Japanese American poets on any syllabus or reading list, none were mentioned in class. It could have been construed from their absence that they were not relevant to the study of poetry. The tradition by which I was meant to understand myself was predominantly white, European American. If I was going to have a relationship with non-white poetry, especially by Asian Americans, especially by Japanese Americans, those relationships would have to be fugitive—trysts.

The Mansfield Library was named after Senator Mike Mansfield. Statues of him and his wife Maureen stand in a small grove of trees in front of the library, Mansfield gazing into campus with cryptic determination, Maureen gazing worshipfully, yet apprehensively, at him. Mansfield served on the board that interrogated the Issei at Fort Missoula. I could not go to the library without being forced to feel that same gaze pressing into my grandfather, and the gazes of all the hoary white men who believed, as Mansfield did, in their ability and authority to assess the fitness of a Japanese man to be free.

Poetry was in the basement. I never saw anyone. I was always alone. I discovered, down there, in that solitude, my first Japanese American poets: Mitsuye Yamada, Lawson Fusao Inada, Janice Mirikitani, all of whom were incarcerated—Yamada as a teenager in Minidoka, Inada as a young child in Jerome and Amache, Mirikitani as an infant in Rohwer. Their names glowed on the spines. Time froze, flowed backwards. I sat on the floor, and floated into the attention of these uncanny poets, their voices close, more precise.

In the introduction to *Legends from Camp*, Inada, sitting in a petrified forest on a summer night, shares a "simple show-and-tell" about Japanese American history, using stones scattered around the forest as reference points. "For starters," he writes, "let's say these rocks over here are Japan. And this smooth one where we're standing—with the sand on it, see?—is Amache, in the Colorado desert, not all that far from here. While we're at it, let's let that little stone by your foot stand in for Leupp—a 'mini-camp' right here on the Navajo Nation. (And, yes, we had major camps on other reservations; so you might say that it makes sense that the chief camps administrator went on to become chief of the Bureau of Indian Affairs, where he 're-deployed' his policy of 'relocation.' Which included, yes, 'termination.' Which reminds me—down the ridge, in Europe, our relatives had base camps in Italy, France, Germany, and some of them liberated a camp called Dachau.)"[121]

In Mitsuye Yamada's "Search and Rescue," an old man, thought to be "out of his head," wanders beyond the barbed wire fence and disappears. A search party goes out. Yamada describes the "feel of freedom" of following the man's "twisted trail" through "gnarled knuckles" of greasewood. Where did he go? Maybe he was not "out of this head"—maybe he was not even old—but in his right mind, leaving behind him a "twisted trail" to throw the search off. Maybe he was trying to get free.[122]

---

121. Lawson Fusao Inada, *Legends from Camp* (Minneapolis: Coffee House Press, 1992)

122. When I told Mitsuye that the first poem of hers that I read was "Search and Rescue," she said, as if no time had passed, "They found him dead. There was a storm. He was half-buried." The playwright Nikki Nojima Louis, who was four or five at the time, remembers the search party, the "muffled and shouted voices of panic and concern, the discovery of his body in that vast landscape outside of block 44, where I lived. It was the last block in camp."

Years later, at the end of a tour of Minidoka, Anna Tamura, of the National Park Service, who had led thirty of us for several hours around the sacred grounds, asked if anyone had any final questions. "I do," said Mike Ishii. "My great-uncle was found dead on the edge of camp, do you know where that was?" "Four miles away," Anna said, knowing immediately who Ishii was talking about. "He went out looking for greasewood." Greasewood was a prized possession in camp, especially pieces that were, as Mitsuye wrote, gnarled, because the wood, twisted into phenomenal shapes and polished to a shine, made beautiful objects. Ishii's great-uncle, Takaji Edward Abe, was one of those who went out to

In "Shadow in Stone," Mirikitani visits Hiroshima (August 1984), wanders along the Motoyasu, the tributary of the Ota nearest to where the atomic bomb detonated. "The river speaks," she writes, then the river speaks. "I received the bodies / leaping into my wet arms," the river says. People, on fire and melting, jumped or fell into the water and died, many of them immediately, against each other. "I seek solace in the stone," Mirikitani continues, "with human shadow burned into its face." The bomb emitted a flash so bright, it imprinted people's shadows onto the ground. A man sitting on the steps of a bank, for example, waiting for the bank to open, his memory made permanent on the steps. "I want to put my mouth to it," Mirikitani writes. I was shocked by the nakedness of her desire to kiss or breathe life into a shadow, but what was more shocking? "The Americans / have licked the core / of your inner organ!" wrote Seishu Hozumi, tanka poet, hibakusha.[123]

I visited Hiroshima for the first time when I was ten. My sister (13) and I walked along the Motoyasu, the reflection of the skeletal Genbaku Dome wavering in the black-green water. I do not remember my parents. They were there, they brought us, it was their idea, where were they? The question seemed to be: what does it mean to be American? Or, what does America mean? Or, what does America do? Or, what does it mean to be you?

"The atomic bomb was part of incarceration," Emiko Omori said. She and her sister Chizu, both of whom were incarcerated in Poston, were visiting my class—Literature of Japanese American Incarceration, Colorado College (2023).

---

collect greasewood. He went with a friend, December 1, 1942. They got separated. A snowstorm blew through, so thick that Abe could not see where he was going.
123. *Outcry from the Inferno: Atomic Bomb Tanka Anthology*, edited and translated from the Japanese by Jiro Nakano (Honolulu: Bamboo Ridge Press, 1990)

We watched their documentary, *Rabbit in the Moon*, the day before. We talked about the processes of dehumanization at which the United States excels, and how the dehumanization of the Japanese American community helped shape the national disposition towards the atomic bombings of Hiroshima and Nagasaki into a debate over whether or not the mass murder of over one hundred thousand people *in an instant*—the spontaneous release of a million suns; the incineration, first thing in the morning, of children on the banks of the Motoyasu—was "justified."

Rabbit in the Moon begins with Emiko Omori speculating on why she did not have children. Over images of children holding hands in a circle, twirling parasols, playing with a dog, eating noodles in highchairs, Omori says, "Like me, my child would be an American, trapped in the body of an unwanted alien race. Could I conceal from my child how I wished he or she was more white, so as not to suffer the rejection I had just because of my face?"

This question, and these images, are preceded by a story about stones: "In the 1950s a Wyoming farmer unearthed a 55-gallon oil drum on land that was formerly a World War II concentration camp. It had been buried by the inmates. It was filled with hundreds of small river stones…each one carefully inscribed with a Japanese character…coming to light like fragments of memory."

The story is also told in the final pages of both Karen Ishizuka's *Lost & Found: Reclaiming the Japanese American Incarceration* and Duncan Ryuken Williams's *American Sutra: A Story of Faith and Freedom in the Second World War*. Bureau of Reclamation, operating a road grader near the cemetery, hit the oil drum. There were almost two thousand stones. They were given to the white couple who owned the land (Nora and Les Bovee), who gave them as gifts to people who visited Heart Mountain. "They were my guiding light," Emiko Omori told me, about the stones.

"Whenever I waivered or wanted to throw in the towel when working on *Rabbit*, the little stones kept me going."

According to *American Sutra*, two Japanese scholars determined that the characters on the stones were written by Nichikan Murakita, a Buddhist priest and master calligrapher, who was incarcerated with his wife, Masako, in Heart Mountain. They determined that Murakita had written one character per stone, the Scripture of the Blossom of the Fine Dharma, the Lotus Sutra.

In "Picking Up Stones," Lawson Inada tells the story of another Buddhist priest, Nyogen Senzaki, also incarcerated in Heart Mountain, who:

> went about gathering pebbles
> and writing words on them—
> common words, in Japanese
> with a brush dipped in ink.
>
> Then he'd return them
> to their source, as best he could

Other incarcerees made a game out of gathering Senzaki's stones, but:

> it was difficult to tell
> which was which:
>
> "his" pebbles, just plain pebbles,
> or those of which, in his hands,
> had remained mute,
> dictating silence…

In her poem "The Well," Amy Uyematsu suggests that the stones were not the work of a single individual, but were

each inscribed
by a different hand,
each crying out. [124]

And that each stone was inscribed with something different: the name of a person, a family, a single kanji

snow   wind   cold   sky
shame   home   bird. [125]

The Bovees donated the rest of the stones to JANM. A man named Shinjiro Kanazawa wrote a letter to the museum saying that the stones were written by the parents of deceased children and should be treated accordingly. "When a child died," Ishizuka writes, paraphrasing Kanazawa, "grieving parents would write passages from sutras—and sometimes their children's names—on pebbles and build the stones into piles in order to help the deceased safely enter the other world."

There is a place children go when they die that is filled with stones of infinite color, shape and design. Sai no Kawara, the Dry Bed of the River of Souls. When the children find themselves—abandoned, bewildered—in the Dry Bed of the River of Souls, they begin, instinctively, to gather stones which they build, instinctively, into towers. It is only after building towers of stones that the children are able to achieve their afterlife. That is the instinct: the afterlife is inborn. But the children are not alone. With them in the Dry Bed of the River of Souls are demons who knock over the towers, scatter the stones. The demons appear, in sixteenth century scrolls, red-hot and naked, with horns, fangs,

---

124. Amy Uyematsu, "The Well," *Nights of Fire, Nights of Rain* (Los Angeles: Story Line Press, 1997)
125. Ibid.

and hooves, wielding iron clubs, wild manes whipping back, eyes pulling at their nerves, but that is not, or not exactly, how the demons appeared in the twentieth century, and that is not how they are appearing in the twenty-first. The children, however—and however terrorized they are—are undeterred, and keep gathering stones, keep building towers, keep striving, together and alone, to cross the threshold out of the underworld and into the afterlife.

"To live in Zen," said Senzaki, in his final dharma lecture (June 16, 1957), "you must watch your steps minute after minute, closely. As I have always told you, you should be mindful of your feet."[126]

I was invited by Williams to write a response to Senzaki's poetry for a book he was editing on the subject of religion in camp: *Sutra and Bible: Faith and the Japanese American World War II Incarceration*, a companion to an exhibition of the same name at JANM. I did not know that Senzaki wrote poems, but of course he did. The act of "gathering pebbles" and writing "common words" on them, then returning them to their "source," is one definition, maybe one of the clearest, of poetry. Here is the poem that I wrote:

126. Nyogen Senzaki, *Like a Dream, Like a Fantasy: The Zen Teachings and Translations of Nyogen Senzaki* (Boston, MA: Wisdom Publications, 2005)

THE EMPTY HANDS
for/after Nyogen Senzaki

I cannot help
but see
and yet struggle to see
in Nyogen Senzaki's poems

faces
floating

along the body
of a snake

black, winding away
from the spring flower
blooming in

America,

that is
the ritual effacement

of those whose faces
I cannot help
but see

in ours, in yours
in my own

floating along the body
of a silent, surreptitious snake

like scales, like sequins, shining
suns

like suns
shining into

the future
with the shades drawn

That is where we, the descendants, are
and where we will always be

Beckoning them
with the empty hands

of those from whom everything was taken

Faces
separated
from their bodies

bodies arrested, separated
into phases

that constitute what passes
for history

There is no such thing

There is teaching. There is learning
There is heaven, earth

but history? There is no such thing

if the light of a face
if the light of many thousands of faces
takes generations to reach us

and to be seen
clearly
and to not even be seen, clearly

but as a figurative concentration

there is no such thing

There is teaching, there is learning
that is heaven, *that* is earth

that is the endless reconstitution of faces
into the meaning and the order
of independence
in between

heaven and earth, *the empty hands*

open, and introduce
their emptiness as sanctuary

but, as the scripture of a harder-won fate
will have it,

cannot be filled, cannot be taken
or even touched

by the lives—by the faces
rising off the winding body

and to which they are held out
to which they are conditioning
their beneficent and beautiful atmosphere
to hold

The empty hands
must remain

empty
or they are not

THE WOODEN BUILDING WILL BE LEFT FOR THE ANGEL'S REVENGE

IN THE FIRST CHAPTER OF *THE GRAVE ON THE WALL*, I wrote about visiting the town where my grandfather was born (Oko, Kurahashi, Hiroshima), but I have thought, many times since—and I thought it then too—that I was mistaken, that it was not the town where my grandfather was born, but a place I had conjured out of reading too intently a glimmer of information in my grandmother's unfinished journal. I could not tell which feeling grounded me more fully in being there: that I was in the exact place where my grandfather was born or that I had traveled thousands of miles and one hundred years to a place that was perfectly unrelated.

Angel Island reminds me of the Inland Sea. The wind, the trees, the sun off the water. Traveling a short distance from the mainland yet feeling ages away. Feeling protected by the sea while the sea bears down on the bodies it conceals. The stones in the small graveyard on the hill overseeing boats as they disappear into the mirage from which islands hang upside-down. Cicadas, loud, the sound of the sun. The eucalyptus smelled, the day I visited Angel Island, in August, like they were burning. There were holes in the leaves, insects chewing the cliffs from Perimeter Road down to where immigrants first set foot in the United States. The country might have appeared, from the boat, and the opening of the Bay, like a country of islands.

"Angel Island...pretty name, ne?" says Mrs. Kawamura in *Come See the Paradise*. She is upstairs in the house her family has been ordered to leave and is feeding letters into a fire in a trash can. Lily, her eldest daughter (Tamlyn Tomita), joins her. Mrs. Kawamura (Shizuko Hoshi) tells Lily about arriving in the United States. "When I first got off the steamer, all I had was the clothes I was wearing, a small bag, a pretty hat, and a parasol." A lifetime later, she is still being forced to parcel out, fast, the entirety of her existence.

"Angel Island is a wound covered in plaque," writes Claire Hong, in *Upend*. The first thing I heard about Angel Island was that there was a hospital and that it was haunted. It was fenced off. A sign said it was under renovation, that it would reopen as a museum in 2016. It was August 2017. Ten million dollars had been spent, four million remained of the budget, but there was no evidence of where the millions had gone. The hospital was swaying.

I visited Angel Island for the haunted hospital and the immigration station, but when I got there, I turned away, walked back up the hill to Perimeter Road, wandered onto a promontory of tall grass. The North Garrison of Fort McDowell ran from Perimeter Road to the cliff. The barracks were demolished in 1973. Piles of sun-bleached wood were scattered in the grass. A sign had fallen over. "KEEP," it said. "OUT," "GOING," or "TAKE IT"? A handcart overflowed with power tools, foam sealant, paint, hundreds of rusted nails, bags of concrete split open, the concrete hardened with seasons of rain. An enormous machine, wrapped with a bright green hose, said, "LeRoi." Some project had been initiated, but there were no signs, outside the detritus, of what it might have been. All the trees had been cut down, all the equipment and hardware had been hauled out to the promontory, but there were no structures, no foundation.

I climbed over a fence and walked back down to the immigration station. The grounds were adorned with benches, dedicated by the families of immigrants who passed through. White immigrants, hours. Non-white, non-Chinese immigrants, including the Japanese, days. Chinese immigrants, weeks, even months. I imagined children and grandchildren walking the grounds looking for the most meaningful view. The benches that did not face the water, but less scenic views, the road or a fence, reminded me of the elderly woman riding a bus in Osamu Dazai's "One Hundred Views of Mount Fuji," who, when everyone turns their head to look out the windows at the mountain, "stared out the opposite window at the cliff."[127]

Two benches in the Asian Man's Recreation Yard sat close together. They shared a view of the chain-link fence, the prison yard through it. Men played volleyball, stood along the fence and watched. Women and children were permitted beyond the fence, accompanied by a guard. White immigrants were permitted everything. Their rooms were private, spacious, their food was delicious. They were not confined to a yard, but to what was called the "European Playground."

The sign at the entrance to the immigration station begins: "Although it is often compared to Ellis Island, Angel Island was not a place of welcome." Ellis Island held over six hundred Japanese immigrants on the east coast between December 1941 and June 1944. The facility where they were detained opened six days *before* Pearl Harbor.

---

127. Osamu Dazai, "One Hundred Views of Mount Fuji," *Early Light*, translated from the Japanese by Ralph McCarthy (New York: New Directions, 2022)

The Chinese and Japanese men were detained on the second floor at Angel Island. The windows of Room 206 faced uphill, with a view of eucalyptus and evergreens. The room used to be larger, but a partition cut it in half. The windows facing the sea were painted black. The room was filled with bunk beds, three beds high, six per unit, each unit held together by poles up the middle. They looked like beanstalks. The room held one hundred men, dozens beyond capacity. The sunlight sifted through the eucalyptus into the room, was granular on the wood floor. When the men arrived, there were no mattresses.

A sign hanging from a bed frame said INSTALLATION IN PROGRESS. Two young men dressed in white were lying on beds. I thought they were sleeping. When they began unfurling their limbs, I hid behind a post. A woman, also in white, entered the room. "Do you want feedback?" she asked. I thought she was talking to me and began, confusedly, to answer, when the men stopped unfurling and said, "How did that look?"

They got off the beds and followed the woman through a door. Chinese Men's Recreation Room. Two men were sitting at a table in the dark, maniacally shuffling mahjongg tiles, which popped like wet wood in a fire. Two men stood on opposite ends of a ping-pong table covered with hundreds of balls, but the men were not moving, and the tension of their stillness made the balls look like they were about to hatch. The men, as dancers, were incarnating—summoning—spirits. And even though the immigrants did not die in these rooms, some part of them stayed.

Another man stood facing the wall, making calligraphic gestures with his hand. The immigration station is famous for the poetry the Chinese immigrants carved into the walls. The walls were repainted eight times, but the poems persisted, flowering through the paint. They were written by immigrants who were detained the longest or were awaiting deportation. They carved the characters with their bodies. "The poets must have stayed long to carve the words so well," writes Maxine Hong Kingston, in *China Men*. They confessed to having spent fortunes to reach the "Land of the Flowery Flag," only to be detained on the "lonely island." The poems record the sound of insects at night, wild geese, the waves, "angry surf." "Who was to know that I would be imprisoned at Devil's Pass?" wrote an anonymous poet. "There is no flower beneath my pillow, and my dreams are not sweet," wrote another. "I wish to go back to the motherland," another. "If the land of the Flowery Flag is occupied by us in turn / The wooden building will be left for the angel's revenge."[128]

"I just sensed there were unhappy feelings, or maybe spirits," Sherri Inenaga told me, about her visit to Angel Island. Her parents and grandparents, on both sides, were incarcerated in Walerga and Tule Lake, and she had an uncle on Angel Island.

"I got out of the building quickly," she said.

"What building?" I asked.

"In the room that had the writings on the wall, and the women's dorms. My uncle told me that there was a ghost on Angel Island and either he or one of his friends had woken in the middle of the night screaming and felt like he was being choked, but no one was there. And I either read about or my aunt told me about a woman who had committed suicide while being held on Angel Island. She poked a chopstick in her head through her ear."

Did she mean Hom Wong Shee? Was there another?

"I cannot recall if the incident happened to my uncle or to his brother," Inenaga continued, "but I remember him telling me about it when I was maybe eight. He said the

---

128. *Island: Poetry and History of Chinese Immigrants on Angel Island, 1910-1940*, eds. Him Mark Lai, Genny Lim, Judy Yung (Seattle: University of Washington Press, 2014)

ghost was on the person's chest, choking him, and that it had happened to others."

The artist Emily Hanako Momohara camped for three days and two nights on Angel Island. She visited once before, with her father. Her great-grandfather passed through when he immigrated from Ehime, but his records were destroyed in the fire. Momohara asked how long, on average, Japanese immigrants were detained. Three days and two nights, she was told. She returned alone. It rained and was windy. Her tent leaked. During the day she collected plants, flowers, ferns, pinecones, leaves, stones, bark, which she kept dry in a food safe. At night, she arranged what she collected into what she calls "islands" and photographed them on a picnic table. She lit them with a flashlight. They were homages to kakejiku, hanging scrolls, and to her grandmother, who practiced bonsai and ikebana, and had aspirations of becoming an artist.

Angel Island (2014). The islands, illuminated in circles of light and surrounded by deep, evocative darkness, transform on their small, wet stage: dark purple flowers on reed-like stalks into dancers swooning or bending from the force of unseen, slow-motion violence; dry pine needles sticking up from a broken seed packed with dirt and flower buds into those same dancers but with arms raised in triumph, waving hello or goodbye; light purple flowers tucked into a thick piece of bark into a body at rest, curled up, maybe dreaming. The imagination of a life in a distant, obscure, yet ingrained and inescapable place, one which seems to be hovering just below the horizon, like the sun the moment after it descends out of sight into color.

The men in white who were moving, stopped moving, and the men who were not moving, moved. Three women looked on, every so often asking a question or giving an instruction.

I stood in the doorway. One of the men came up behind me, saw my notebook, and whispered: "Researching the ancestors." Was it a question? Was he asking me if I was researching the ancestors? Or was he telling me that is what they were doing? The dancers moved with a fluidity that suggested that they were making a home, however troubled it might be. Not ghosts, but the illumination and the coming to life of the shadows.

I walked back up to Perimeter Road. My memory of the women and men in the dark rooms was of plants spiraling, reaching for light. Angels. I felt the sun off the water, the trees, the wind. The presence of someone behind me. I thought—feared, for some reason—that if I turned around they would disappear. I felt alone, but with them. I kept repeating to myself what the man had said: "researching the ancestors, researching the ancestors." I repeated the words so many times, they became phenomenal, until I was no longer sure if the man had said "researching" or if what he had actually said was "rehearsing." Because they were doing that too.

I must have taken the ferry back to the mainland, but I do not remember reboarding. I only remember approaching the island. My memory ends on Perimeter Road. Eucalyptus, feeling someone behind me. Wanting to look back, not wanting to look back. On the island, *rehearsing the ancestors.*

RESEARCHING THE ANCESTORS

What is an ancestor? What is your relationship with them?

"A dead person you love," said my daughter, Yumi Taguchi Schumaier Shimoda (4 at the time).

"My beginning," said Joni Kimoto.

"The web through time that binds us to the beginning," said Elán Rie.

"The love that binds and transforms," said Mike Ishii.

"A chorus of voices that speak to me in tiny hints," said Katie Kamio.
   "Through dreams, intuition and signs," said Lauren Miura.
   "Using very little written or verbal language," said Jennifer Mie Oda. "A gesture or a look, or a placement in a photograph."

"I feel called out to in some moments," said Lyn Ishizaki-Brown, "like when I glance at the clock and see the time I was born."

"Their voices chant and sing deep in my psyche and my soul," said Rick Noguchi.

"Someone whose energy I feel passing through me," said Mia Ayumi Malhotra.

"A spiritual energy that lives in my mind and soul," said Shizu Saldamando.

"A kindred spirit," said Tiffani Koyano.

"The sweet spirit that gives me life and purpose," said Sharon Yamato.

"I like to think of the spirits of all my dead as leftover electrical impulse expelled from the body," said Madeleine Mori.

"I have ancestors of blood and bone, spirit, place, vocation, queerness, movement," said Casey Hidekawa Lane/Levinski.

"I picture a Bon Odori dance," said Kimiko Guthrie, "colorful, joyous energy moving fluidly around in an enormous circle."

"Guardian angels," said Susan Kamei.

"Benevolent ghosts," said Rea Tajiri.

"I see and feel a whole host of living/active ghosts with names I don't know passing in and out of the earth-plane," said Brynn Saito.

"They are infinite in number and spread across continents and contain infinite experiences," Shizu Saldamando continued.

"Fragments of my brain," said Kiyoko Merolli. "Like they're in there, watching me, and my every move."

"My conscience," Rick Noguchi continued.

228

"Ancestors are stories," said Morgan Ome.

"Stories I'm told and stories I tell myself," said Ana Iwataki.

"Someone you are linked to through a shared story," said Jessica Kashiwabara, "whose life you continue to live through your own."

"We are a part of their stories," Elán Rie continued, "and they are a part of ours."

"A way of living in narrative," said Vince Schleitwiler, "wondering about the distance between their lives and mine, and whether imagining my life as a continuation of their story can give me some other ways of being and acting in the world."

"I have to answer to them in the way I think and act," said Suzy Nakamura.

"In my work as an artist, I've tried to express this sense that past is present is future," said Sandra Honda. "The thread that stitches past to present to future is memory embodied in stories and the emotions flowing from them. In these ways, ancestors are time and the lessons left by them, if we are smart enough to listen."

"Memories that I did not know I had that come unbidden," said Patrick Hayashi.

"ANCESTRY is deeply attached to LEGACY, which is rooted in HISTORY and inextricably tied to STORYTELL-ING, the most venerable & sustainable of the ARTS," said Nikki Nojima Louis.

"A relationship, a link, and a legacy," said George Uba.

"I believe in legacy burdens," said Kristen Amaral. "We carry the burdens of our ancestors in our bones and it is up to us to heal them."

"We carry ancestral contexts within which we must work, and which we must work to heal," said Dee (Tomiyama) Black.

"A gift and a responsibility," Ana Iwataki continued.

"We can treasure what they gifted us," writes Jami Nakamura Lin, in *The Night Parade*, "while also acknowledging that in certain cases they did not tell us enough, or that what they said was wrong, or was right for that time and place but needs to change now."

"The more that a person grows and heals, the less of their own loss and trauma they inflict on future generations and the more room they allow for positive energy to infiltrate their descendants," said Amy Lee-Tai. "This isn't to say that a person is bound by the history and actions of their ancestors, simply that descendants inherit tendencies and then make autonomous choices which, together, help compose a life."

"A reminder that the historical is personal," said Lauren Sumida.

"A way to reflect on family history, produce pride in one's roots and culture, and feel grateful for the sacrifices and decisions they made," said Mina Loy Akira Checel.

"They remind us of our roots, how we came to be, and who we might be in the future," Morgan Ome continued.

"My roots, my tree trunk, my base," said Joni Kimoto.

"The roots of our existence," said Julie Abo.

"From *kānaka maoli* who are relatives and friends, I've learned that the earth itself, *'āina*, is an ancestor as well, and try to pay reverence in ways I can, mostly in my own poetry," said Garrett Hongo. "As a Japanese American, I cannot claim the scores of generations on the land that the indigenous can, so my devotion is encircled and even cautioned by a conscious humility and deference, not only to the land itself, but to the *kupuna*, elders who are the Native Hawaiian people."

"Anyone who has existed on Earth before me," said Kay Yatabe.

"Like the kami in a house or in a tree," said Tamiko Nishita-Hawkinson.

"I see trees as my ancestors too," Dee (Tomiyama) Black continued.

"Someone told me once that, for me, true romantic partnership looks like two trees in a forest," Ana Iwataki continued. "That's probably the most lucid image I have of what it might mean to be an ancestor."

"Ancestors also carry cultures," said Chizu Omori. "The way one's mind was educated to think and to accept certain norms and values."

"A catalyst, a guide, a ground," Ana Iwataki continued.

"They tend to talk when I need guidance," said Brett Esaki.

"They guide me in finding out more about them so the day we meet again I will recognize them," said Jennifer Fukutomi Lee.

"They reunite people," said Erin Shigaki.

"To commune with the ancestors is also to grapple with who they might have been as people," said Sara Onitsuka.

"To always remember that they were people who were as complicated and contradictory as the people who populate my current reality," said Maggie Tokuda-Hall, "full of joy and resentments and inconsistencies and faults."

"I live with their wounds, their shame, their proclivities," Mia Ayumi Malhotra continued. "Their reactions to danger or fearful situations."

"I share their blood, their traumas, their joys," said Alyssa Watanabe Kapaona.

"I know that my ancestors travel my bloodline," said Fred Sasaki, "and that trauma is archived in our DNA.

"I wonder how much of my hurt and rage belong to them—to all of us," Brynn Saito continued.

"Sometimes I think that I feel all the anger they couldn't," said Alexandra Arai Cauley.

"I believe we're feedback loops," Fred Sasaki continued.

"I feel linked to the women in my ancestral line through childbirth, through pain and sorrow, through the sadness we have all been steeped in since conception," Mia Ayumi Malhotra continued, "through amniotic fluid, breast milk, tears. I mother my own daughters with a sense of this weighty, inherited sadness."

"A definition rooted in the chosen family of queerness," said Emily Mitamura.

"I have been seeking queer nikkei ancestors and looking for subtle traces of their same-sex intimacies and defiance of gender norms," said TT Takemoto. "I feel kinship with these ancestors and think of them as my chosen family of queer aunts and uncles."

"Someone who made the people who made me," said Emily Nakashima. "Or made the people who made the people who made me, backward as far as you can go. I mean *made* both in the literal biological sense, but I also include other major acts of nurturing, teaching, feeding, and supporting. Anyone who substantially helped the generations of my family before me survive and thrive."

"Someone who laid the foundation for us to arrive," said Heather Nagami.

"Who set the stage for my chances in life," said Karen Kiyo Lowhurst.

"Those that have gone through grief for my family to exist," said Karli Ikeda-Lee.

"The key to my survival," Heather Nagami continued.

"The sacrifice, to me, connects us," Mina Loy Akira Checel continued.

"Is an ancestor a being whose steps shaped the paths we walk?" said Sean Miura. "Is an ancestor the path itself? Is an ancestor simply the instruction—*walk down this path*? Can we stray from the path? Are we forever in relation to the path? Is there a path?"

"They are always in front of me leading the way," Suzy Nakamura continued.

"If we are in opposition to our ancestors can we reconcile that?" Sean Miura continued. "Can we move beyond the fortresses they built? If we can never destroy those fortresses (them being in the past) how much can we really disregard them?"

"I wonder how complicit my ancestors might have been in Japan's brutality and war crimes," Sara Onitsuka continued.

"You are not culpable for your ancestors' crimes," said Elizabeth Fugikawa, "but you are responsible for the legacy of those crimes (particularly in terms of colonialism and genocide) and must strive to do better so that your descendants will live in a better world."

"I think of activists and regular people who resisted state-sanctioned violence or heteronormativity or any of the cruelties done upon the historically disempowered through protest or noncompliance as my ancestors as well," Maggie Tokuda-Hall continued.

"I feel most connected to them when I feel my blood rising," Sara Onitsuka continued, "when I have that familiar feeling of perceiving an injustice occurring. Then I speak and move with the weight of my ancestors."

"My sense of responsibility comes from my connection to all ancestors committed to justice, community, and care," said Miya Sommers, "that my lineage and my future is embedded in an ecosystem of generations of relationships."

"The ancestors provide the fire in my veins," Sara Onitsuka continued.

"A relation who, if you lived contemporaneously, would claim you as one of their people or would show up to support you," said Allison Hana Fischer-Olson.

"The home of protection, warnings, and generational curses," said Kristin Kamoto.

"They help avert major disasters," Erin Shigaki continued.

"When I think about my relationship to my ancestors, I think of people whose faces I can almost see and whose voices I can almost hear," said Erin Aoyama.

"Though I may not know their faces, their names, or the sounds of their voices, through the moments of encounter,

I come into contact with them, and their hearts (心) live on," said Koji Lau-Ozawa.

"But there is also a sense of the ancestors as something far more intangible, like the parts of us that are ancient, or an infinite compassion," said Starr Miyata.

"I imagine a nebulous cloud where all the ancestors drift," said Anna Kimura.

"They are available to me when I feel the need to find answers or support," said Marlene Shigekawa.

"Sometimes answers but more often ways into questions," Erin Aoyama continued.

"I can only come up with more questions," Sean Miura continued.

"Because of my ancestors, I am more than myself," said Katherine Terumi Laubscher.

"It is a connection to a sense of self that is larger than myself, a collective identity that is more powerful for being shared," Maggie Tokuda-Hall continued.

"They are also the people who come after me," said Nina Yoshida Nelsen.

"Their deaths brought to light what is left when we leave," Suzy Nakamura continued.

"That we are the stalks on branches reaching from them towards the end," Elán Rie continued.

REHEARSING THE ANCESTORS

Where do the ancestors gather? And where do you go to be with them?

"In the morning," said Sesshu Foster.

"When I look in the mirror," said Satsuki Ina.

"In me," said Masami Okahara Chin.

"Within me," said Emiko Omori.

"Always within me," said Ken Mochizuki.

"Within myself," said Karli Ikeda-Lee

"In myself and outside of myself," said Tiffany Koyama Lane

"At my back, beyond my reach, in my body and all around me," said Casey Hidekawa Lane/Levinski.

"Around me all the time," said Tiffani Koyano.

"Hovering around us all the time," said Tosh Tanaka.

"In us," said Eric Kubota.

"Within you," said Lisa Nori Nishimura Pawin.

"I go inside and outside of my mind to visit them," said Heather Nagami. "Sometimes I talk to them, and when I do, I feel like I'm inside and outside at once."

"Floating around the edges of my consciousness," said Laura Mariko Cheifetz.

"In my imagination," said Marlene Shigekawa.

"In my mind or heart," said Brittany Arita.

"In the hearts and minds of those that think of them and feel their presence," said Katie Fujiye Nuss Louis.

"All my Ancestors are seated in the luminous center, my Heart, my connection to and expression of Heart Fire and Fire of the Universe," said Mike Ishii. "My luminous center is where I connect to my Ancestors. From my luminous center I ascend to Baihui (100 Ancestors) in my crown and from there to Heaven where they always await me."

"In my blood," said Sara Onitsuka.

"In my mitochondrial DNA," said Linda Suzu Kawano.

"Somewhere up there in the ether," said Alden Hayashi.

"In the air, in the water, the soil," said Chelsey Oda.

"In our earth," said Esther Honda.

"In nature," said Ellen Bepp.

"Where there is nature and stillness," said Alyssa Watanabe Kapaona.

"Where there are stones and gardens," said Nancy Ukai.

"Near a stream," said Autumn Yamamoto.

"In moments of quiet reflection," said Evan Iwata.

"In little moments of noticing," said Megan Kowta.

"My grandparents raised me with the notion that everything is *alive* in nature, holding a spirit, and where I can commune with my ancestors," Ellen Bepp continued.

"My parents raised me in a house in a valley surrounded by forests and hills," said Naomi Kubota Lee. "Fog drifted in from the ocean and we had a creek with wandering salamanders. It was a way to get away from it all. It gave them

238

peace. And now I feel that was the point. This is where I visit their souls."

"Meditation," said Kay Yatabe.
    "In Thusness," said Karen Ishizuka.

"I have come to realize that communion with my ancestors for me is a deeply intellectual practice," said Maggie Tokuda-Hall. "It's something I do through reasoning and questioning and looking for meaning"

"Inward thinking," said Kyle Shoji Toyama.
    "In my thoughts," said Rick Noguchi.
    "In my thoughts and memories," said Nikki Nojima Louis.
    "In our memories of them," said Kristine Aono. "These memories become history we pass on to successive generations, helping to define ourselves and our place in this continuum."

"I most often visit with my ancestors when I'm not thinking about it," said Erin Aoyama. "Maybe because I spend so much time thinking about them, it's the moments when I'm less involved in my own thoughts that I can be with them."

"We were in sitting in a cemetery one afternoon having a picnic with my grandmother," said Rea Tajiri. "We lit incense over one of the graves. My grandmother said that when she was young, she got lost in the woods in Japan on her way to bringing the cattle in. She said that a fox appeared and showed her the way home. My aunt explained that in Japan, foxes were magical animals and that they could be bad and play mean tricks, or be benevolent. I remember saving the incense in a tiny matchbox for years."

"In spaces of ritual and remembrance," Casey Hidekawa Lane/Levinski continued.

"We see them every day on the altar," said Dori Shimoda.

"I have a little altar in my home with incense, fruit, my father's ashes," said Jami Nakamura Lin.

"When I light the green incense sticks and place them in front of the altar," said Morgan Ome, "when I strike the *rin* and hear it ring."

"I can feel them settle when I close my eyes at the sound of a deep, round bell," said Sean Miura.

"When I touch the beads and the candle goes out," said Brian Komei Dempster.

"During *obon* season," Ellen Bepp continued, "when I dance in the festivals to welcome my ancestors' spirits back."

"At Bon Odori gatherings," said Tamiko Nimura, "in the fans unfurled, the waves of raised arms, the circles of dancers, the gentle bobbing of the paper lanterns.

"The minister at my temple says that at Obon our ancestors come sit on the porch or outside of our homes because they don't want to intrude too much, just check in to say hi," said Lisa Doi.

"They check in on family members who are still living but they also travel the world and have their own interests," said Julie Kanazawa.

"I do Buddhist chanting for my ancestors," said Kimiko Guthrie, "to thank them, to wish them well on their journeys."

"I feel like the ancestors are free to roam where they wish and are not limited to our finite world," said Maryn Ayumi Masumiya.

"Laying out newspaper at the cemetery in preparation for pouring water over the gravestone and clipping the ends of flower stems," Meri Mitsuyoshi continued, "slicing and twisting konyaku, wearing my grandmother's nenju while chanting at the butsudan, drumming and dancing."

"My family used to go *every weekend* during my childhood to the cemetery to put fresh flowers at the niches of both sets of grandparents," said Paula Fujiwara. "I can go to the cemetery blindfolded—enter the building, climb the stairs to the second floor, turn left, make a U-turn, turn left again and go straight to the niches of my maternal and paternal grandparents and now my parents. It's in my bones."

"The resting places of their bones," said Koji Lau-Ozawa.

"I am still at a point where seeking the ancestors means to wander and try to see and feel and sense the land where they must have once walked," said Starr Miyata.

"In places of historic or communal importance," said Jessica Miyeko Kawamura.

"In places that bring them joy," said Julie Whitecotton.

"The houses and neighborhoods they used to live in," said Valerie Castro.

"At home," said Paul Kitagaki Jr.

"In their belongings that have been passed down," said Evan Iwata.

"An old copper tea kettle, the handle long missing, dug up from under the house," said Willitte Hisami Ishii Herman.

"Whenever I view their photographs, read their letters, build with their tools, eat from their rice bowls," Kristine Aono continued.

"Whenever I touch my grandmother's suitcase from internment," said Danette Godinez.

"When I smell sandalwood," Sean Miura continued.

"My grandma had plants that were descendants of plants that she and relatives brought from Japan," said Miya Sommers. "I think about [Korean American farmer] Kristyn Leach talking about her seed stewardship; she said that seeds carry the generational information of thousands of seasons—embedded in each seed's genealogy carries lessons in survival from each season. I'm reminded of this relationship. So, being in the garden is where I get to be with the ancestors and where I get to be with the gentlest version of myself."

"They gather at the river by the tree," Brian Komei Dempster continued. "They hide in blossoms, the grass hums, *We were here . . . you are one of us*. As we chant the lotus, they bloom again. They gather in stone, crystal bodies chipped, shadow faces on mountains."

"I have felt them coming through as a movement just beyond my peripheral vision, a shadow may flash in my mind, a small noise, a whisper," Willitte Hisami Ishii Herman continued.

"In the collective consciousness of all their living descendants," said Alyxandra Reed-Asakawa.
"In the collective memory of my living relatives, when we share stories and remember them," said Alexis Ajioka.
"I believe they all hang out together talking stories in between watching over us," said Lisa Hernandez.
"In the same area of my mind as the concepts of Identity and Community," said Brett Kodama.

"When their names are known and called," Satsuki Ina continued.

"As long as we keep telling their names and stories," said Benjamin Tomimatsu.

"At unpredictable, spur-of-the-moment times," said Jeanne Sakata, "in my home, my car, alone on a walk, in the company of friends."

"I see them in my family members and the love we all have for each other," said Katharine Ikeda Mascenik.

"Whenever all of the family gathers together to laugh or eat or just have fun in each other's company," said Olivia Kurima.

"When we eat comfort foods," said Corinne Araki-Kawaguchi, "okaii when we're ill, mochi for New Years, senbei with our tea, oyakodonburi, etc."

"They are with us daily as we eat, keeping company with our books, next to me as I cook dinner," Tamiko Nimura continued.

"Over a never-ending meal with loved ones," said Jessica Huey.

"When my granddad was in hospice and couldn't chew food," said Kimiko Tanabe, "we cut up oranges into pieces smaller than a pinky nail and removed the white see-through layer around what seems like the seeds of juice and plated them on small beautiful Japanese plates. My granddad was hovering between the living and the dead. It felt like I was learning or preparing to care for him as an ancestor while he was still living—the labor of preparing and presenting fruit even though he could physically eat very little of it. Was he already an ancestor?"

"Can music be an ancestor?" asked Patrick Hayashi.

"When I listen to or play the taiko drums, I can feel my ancestors resonating in the rhythms," Corinne Araki-Kawaguchi continued.

"When I am playing music, especially free improvisation, I am in this meditative state; it only happens when I'm playing," said Dylan Fujioka.

"I think about them every time I'm about to step on stage," said Nina Yoshida Nelsen.

"I make films about my ancestors," said Renee Tajima-Peña, "and they're gathered in the frames of photographs and films."

"I visit my ancestors in the archives and within my queer speculative films, where I try to create spaces for queer inhabitance and joy," said TT Takemoto.

"Research for making artwork," said Kevin Miyazaki, "finding things like censuses and historic photographs, brings my ancestors to the front of my mind, if only for brief moments."

"When I create art," said Liana Hisako Tai. "The urge to move the brush or sculpt a certain image is how I can be with them, for they were artists and I am one too."

"When I am doing my work (I am a painter)," said Suzanne Kimiko Onodera.

"The artwork is driven by my creative desire to put new things in the world," Kevin Miyazaki continued, "but ultimately acts as a way of preserving the stories of my ancestors."

"What about books?" Patrick Hayashi continued.

"I visit my ancestors every time I sit down to write," said Ruth Sasaki.

"If I slow my mind and am intentional, as with the writing process or meditation process, I can begin to feel them gather with me," said Madeleine Mori.

"Through incorporating details of their lives into a story or even into my *thinking* as if I were writing a story, I feel like I draw closer to them," said Cynthia Kadohata.

"When I write essays and fiction about the Nikkei experience, I do feel the presence of my ancestors looking over my shoulders, which can at times be a bit inhibiting," Alden Hayashi continued.

"My ancestors are alive in my poems," said W. Todd Kaneko.

"They all gather, spirits of blood and spirits of the word, in my poetry," said Garrett Hongo, "gods of emotion and imagination, sponsors of my life."

"My mother's dad drowned during a fishing trip off the coast of Hawaii," Cynthia Kadohata continued. "I know what he looked like because I have a picture, and I know too what she looked like back then. So when she told me that the last words he spoke to her were, *Be a good girl*, it was very easy to picture. If I contemplate this moment as if I were writing about it, it's as if it becomes a memory that I have—as if I actually saw it. This would also be how I would visit with them. It may seem far-fetched, but I believe in some preternatural way we really do meet in this manner."

"Writing is excavation," Ruth Sasaki continued. "I excavate my past, searching for remnants of a civilization that was buried by the incarceration and the atomic bomb, to discover the stories—and the dead live again."

"I raise a picket sign under the sun, and I'm with my ancestors," said Troy Osaki. "I watch an effigy of our president burn. His face melts, and I'm with my ancestors. I hand a bottle of water to the organizer leading us in chants. Our sweaty arms touch, and I'm with my ancestors."

"In bed at night as I fall asleep," Jeanne Sakata continued.

"Dreams," said Ian Martyn. "After my grandmother passed away, I had many dreams about her. Mostly conversations with her, or going places with her like I used to. I still have dreams where she appears, and I enjoy talking to her in them."

"Dreams are described also as leftover electrical impulses in the brain and so it makes sense to me that my dead most often get to visit with me in dreams," Madeleine Mori continued.

"On a plane of existence that is beyond our corporeal and physical world," said Hanako Wakatsuki-Chong. "Perhaps it is an astral plane that also intersects with our world where we can feel their love and support when we gather to remember them."

"I think of them in a sort of spirit plane," Jami Nakamura Lin continued.

"In the spiritual world," said Patrick Shiroishi.

"In a type of spirit world in which they can recall their Earthly lives but are no longer hindered by any of the pain or suffering," Julie Kanazawa continued.

"In the spirit realms; realms of energy and vibration," said Jessica Zanotti.

"In a spiritual realm that is both connected to and beyond this world," Jeanne Sakata continued.

"I want to believe that after we die we reintegrate back into a spiritual realm," said Mitchell Higa, "much like an ocean wave cresting and dissipating back into one ocean."

"The ocean," said Aisuke Kondo.

"The Ocean is a powerful sacred space for me to talk and connect with my Ancestors," said Daryn Wakasa.

"Whenever I'm standing at the edge of the water, I feel very aware that there's an entirely different world beyond where I'm standing, beyond the horizon," said Dylan Mori. "If there is an afterlife, that's where I imagine I will meet my family."

"In the afterlife," said Erin Tsutsumoto.

"I do believe there is some sort of afterlife where all our ancestors are together and observing who and what they have left behind," said Traci Oshiro.

"I don't think of any of them gathering anywhere," said Traise Yamamoto, "as I don't believe that anything other than soulful/spiritual energy and memories survive and circulate, creating another kind of liveness."

"And if my ancestors gather, that is their own affair and I'm not sure I have yet been invited. I feel very much at peace with that," Maggie Tokuda-Hall continued. "It feels to me that I'll be invited at the end of my life, when I will have earned enough perspective to join them."

"I am with my ancestors," said Masako Takahashi.

"They're here," Emiko Omori continued.

"Everywhere," Satsuki Ina continued.

"We visit and talk with our parents more often than when they were alive," Dori Shimoda continued.

"They try to talk to you in the breeze but you don't understand," Karen Ishizuka continued.

"They speak to us—shadows through leaves," Brian Komei Dempster continued.

"Sometimes when leaves amplify them, you almost understand but it's still in a different language," Karen Ishizuka continued.

"I miss not being able to talk to them," Emiko Omori continued.

"You listen anyway," Karen Ishizuka continued. "Listen with all your might."

"Mostly through changes in light," Starr Miyata continued.

"Whenever I take time to look at the moon," said Donna Nagata, "I think of my maternal grandmother."

EPILOGUE

I WILL FOLLOW YOU INTO THE DARK

A FEW MONTHS AGO, MY AUNT RISA CALLED TO SAY
that my grandmother had less than a year to live. We had
no reason not to believe her—my grandmother was turning ninety-seven, had Parkinson's, and had fallen four times
that month, and Risa, who lived thirty minutes from my
grandmother, was the only person in the family taking care
of her—but it was hard to tell, talking to my grandmother
on the computer, that she was dying or might be dead any
minute. She lived in a small room in a nursing home in
the woods west of Baltimore, spent most of her time in a
wheelchair facing a TV she never turned on. A curtain separated her from her roommate, or roommates: a succession
of women who died, were replaced, died, were replaced.
My grandmother was, in that sense, dying.

My mother, my sister, and I flew to Baltimore, then
drove into the woods, to visit my grandmother. To say
goodbye, we said. Her nursing home was called Friends
House. It was established in 1967 by the Religious Society of Friends, the Quakers. Driving the country roads to
Friends House, I told my mother and sister that the Quakers were one of the few communities—the only?—who
stood up for the Japanese Americans during WWII. They
spoke out against removal and incarceration. They visited

the detention centers and camps, sent aid, helped secure the release of thousands of Japanese Americans, opened hostels where they could stay, safely, after camp.

When we got to my grandmother's room, she was sleeping, or looked like it, but when we said her name, she turned and looked at us. Something was up. Why would the three of us be there in her room? My mother, my sister, and I had not been together without our families (Lisa and Yumi, my sister's husband and their daughters) in twenty years, the last time the three of us were alone with my grandmother was in the 1990s, on a trip to Switzerland, I had not seen my grandmother in almost a decade.

It was Saturday. We spent ten hours with my grand-mother—in her room, in a gazebo (where my sister cut my grandmother's hair), in the solarium (where my sister and aunt played the piano; *Dream A Little Dream Of Me*, Richard Marx's *Wherever you go, whatever you do, I will be right here waiting for you*). We took my grandmother to a Japanese restaurant in a strip mall. Mediocre, barely Japanese, but my grandmother—who was the first person to ever make me Japanese food—said it was the best and most beautiful Japanese food she ever had, and I think she meant it. There was only the present. The present was a tunnel. No periphery, no reflection, it was never going to reach light, darkness narrowing to a point. That, anyway, was my idea of what she was experiencing, of how her brain was working and winding down.

I spent ten hours staring at my grandmother's face, trying to see in it the woman I had known, which meant trying to see my grandmother years ago when I was not looking at her as closely and compassionately as I should have been. She, in my effort to reach her in my memory, kept evading me, turning corners. It was confusing trying to remember my grandmother while looking directly at her. Several versions of her were layered behind her face. I was also trying to see in her face, in her eyes, the way she saw me. She knew me, if she knew me at all, when I was young, not yet myself. She knew me less and less as I got older, and probably did not know me very well, if at all, now, and not because of her condition. It had been many years since I had shared my life with her in any but the most passing ways; the look on her face was the reflection of my guilt. She seemed, in a way, beyond death. She was well enough to be driven to a strip mall and seated in front of a plate of sashimi—which is, in the scheme of disintegration, very well. But we had the sense that she was waiting to die, that it was not coming fast enough.

Years earlier, in 1996, after my grandfather died, my grandmother said she wanted to die so she could be with him. Now it was approaching thirty years later and she was still here. On the dresser beneath the TV was a picture frame, face down. My sister picked up the picture: my grandfather, late 1940s. My grandparents were in New York City then, and married, or soon to be. The perils of the West Coast and the asphyxiations of the monstrous, big-sky high desert states, were behind them. Before them: gleaming possibilities. When my sister asked if she wanted it propped up, my grandmother shook her head: no, keep it there. Face down. But what if he wants to see *your* face, I thought. My grandfather called my grandmother *Dimples*.

I said that my grandfather did not write letters to my grandmother from Fort Missoula, which is true. Aside from one short letter my grandfather wrote to his sister-in-law, Hide, which is in his FBI file, there was no record of him having written letters to anyone. But a week before visiting my grandmother, my aunt received, from a cousin I never heard of, an envelope full of additional letters my grandfather wrote to Hide from Fort Missoula. After spending the day with my grandmother, we drove to my aunt's apartment, outside of DC to decompress, and read the letters. There were at least thirty letters, some typewritten, most of them handwritten. I had never seen my grandfather's handwriting before. I had not, until then, read anything he had written, and the idea that he had written anything was, for some naïve, grandchildish reason, unfathomable. All of his letters were written to Hide—his brother's wife, free in Utah. He wrote that he was not allowed to describe the conditions at Fort Missoula—several words and sentences in his letters had been cut out with a scalpel—so his letters were filled with the everyday: meals, naps, baseball, tennis twice a day, movies on Tuesdays. He was taking a class on bookkeeping. An Issei was teaching him how to make geta, which my grandfather was going to send to the women in the family. The Italian and Japanese prisoners put on plays. My grandfather mentioned that he was going to be "Mariko from Little Tokyo." Being in a play was "good medicine," he said. "Can you picture me in such a part?" Among the letters was a postcard *of the prison at Fort Missoula*. As if imprisonment was a vacation, *wish you were here*. White barracks in rows, white buildings across a flat landscape, a river (the Bitterroot) appearing and disappearing off the edge. Was the postcard free—free advertising for the prison—or did my grandfather pay for it? In the lower right corner was a stamp: DETAINED ENEMY ALIEN MAIL EXAMINED. My grandfather reassured Hide he was okay. His letters answered so many of the questions I had about his time in Fort Missoula, more importantly about him—questions I had been asking for years, in the form of descriptions, aching imaginaries. The fact that my aunt had *just* learned about his letters eighty years after he had written them—and after we had both written books about him[129]—and that they were sitting, untouched, in a box in a relative's house, suggested, or confirmed, something both hopeful and depressing: that the realization of

129. Risa Shimoda and Bob Fleshner, *Photographic Memories: A Story of Shinjitsu*, April 2020

a life is often posthumous, that the answers to our most belabored questions about those we love and miss arrive in the form of the mundane voice of the past, waiting for its moment, and for us, in the future, which is so often a time and a place that we, in becoming the loved and the missed, never reach. My grandmother had never seen the letters. She did not know about them. Everything she knew about my grandfather's time in Fort Missoula was from what he told her, which was, of course—as it could only be—a distillation of what he experienced. The person who got closest to knowing what he was doing and thinking *in real time*, was his sister-in-law, Hide, a woman my sister and I never met. Hide put all of that into a box, the box changed hands, many times, and was slid under a bed.

It was getting dark. We read the letters, aloud and to ourselves, excited and in silence. The presence of the past, the revelation of my grandfather's hand moving across thin pieces of paper in the morning, afternoon, night, in a prison that no longer existed but that was, in our hearts and inheritance, everywhere, was too much and somehow not enough. "It's all here," my sister said, crying. I looked at her, and forgot, for a moment, that the letters were not written to *us*, that they had not taken eighty years to reach *us*. And yet, because I am a writer, I believe that maybe they were.

My favorite moment in all of the letters is when, in one of them, after saying goodbye and signing his name, *Shimoda Midori*, my grandfather wrote in the corner, "I'll be waiting for the cherries."

NOTES AND ACKNOWLEDGMENTS

MY GRANDMOTHER (B. 1926) DIED SHORTLY AFTER WE visited her at Friends Home, on October 8, 2023.

"I Will Follow You Into The Dark" is the name of a song performed by Miya Folick.

"How do we memorialize an event that is still ongoing?" is a question Christina Sharpe asks in *In the Wake: On Blackness and Being*, and that is specific to and predicated on the understanding that "chattel slavery and its afterlives are unfolding still." The question has inspired much of my thinking throughout this book, and I am grateful to Sharpe for it.

The choral chapters ("Saving the Incense," "I See The Memory Outline," "You May Not Be On My Time Yet," "Stars Above the Ruins," "To Force Upon Them the Authority of History," "Researching the Ancestors," "Rehearsing the Ancestors") were composed of responses to a questionnaire I shared with over 250 descendants. It consisted of ten questions, ranging from informational to speculative, on the experience of being a descendant. Some of the questions appear at the beginnings of the chapters, some don't. "Researching the Ancestors" and "Rehearsing the

Ancestors" were composed of responses to questions I also asked of survivors. Thank you to everyone who so generously, descriptively, and thoughtfully responded to my questions, and who gifted me permission to include them.

Thank you to everyone who has invited me to give a talk, teach, or write about JA incarceration; the venues, organizations, and publications that have hosted or published me and my work on the subject; and the editors who have made my writing stronger and more clear; much of the writing for this book was generated in response to these invitations and opportunities: Frank Abe and Floyd Cheung (*The Literature of Japanese American Incarceration*, Penguin Classics, 2024), Torran Anderson (Nosotros Academy, Tucson), Dionne Brand and Allison LaSorda (*Brick*), Jason Oliver Chang (Asian and Asian American Studies Institute, UConn), Lawrence-Minh Bùi Davis (Smithsonian Asian Pacific American Center), Lawrence-Minh Bùi Davis and Mimi Khúc (*The Asian American Literary Review*), Thom Donovan (Columbia University), Natalie Diaz (Center for Imagination in the Borderlands, ASU), Yanara Friedland (Fairhaven College), Max Fox and Ava Kofman (*The New Inquiry*), Alan Gilbert and Leigh Marshall (*BOMB*), Sarita Gonzales (University of Arizona), Brandi Katherine Herrera (*Design Week Portland*), Emily Hunt and Brett Fletcher Lauer (Poetry Society of America/International Center of Photography, NYC), Sophia Hussain (The Asian American Writers' Workshop), Kurt Ikeda (Japanese American Museum of Oregon), Deepa Iyer (*Solidarity Is This* podcast), Dorothea Lasky (Columbia University; *Essays*, Essay Press, 2023), Janice Lee (*Entropy*), Angie Sijun Lou and Karen Tei Yamashita (*Dark Soil: Fictions and Mythographies*, Coffee House Press, 2024), Rei Magosaki (Chapman University), Caitie Moore (Thinking Its Presence conference, University of Arizona Poetry Center, 2017), Tamiko Nimura (*Discover Nikkei*), Jeffrey Pethybridge (Jack Kerouac School of Disembodied Poetics, Naropa University),

Jay Ponteri (Pacific Northwest College of Art), Paisley Rekdal (American West Center, University of Utah), Erin Shigaki (Minidoka Pilgrimage, 2023), Patrick Shiroishi (*I was too young to hear silence*, American Dreams Records, 2023), Sandy Sugawara (*Show Me the Way to Go to Home*, Radius Books, 2023), Natasha Varner (Densho), Wakasa Memorial Committee (Town Hall, San Francisco), Duncan Ryuken Williams (*Sutra and Bible*, Kaya Press, 2022), John Yau (*Hyperallergic*), Ariel Yelen (*futurefeed*). Parts of *The Afterlife* were also published in *Literary Hub*, *The Margins*, and *The Nation*; thank you to the editors of those publications.

Research and writing were supported by a Whiting Foundation Creative Nonfiction grant, and a Crown Center Manuscript Seminar grant and a Research and Development grant from Colorado College.

The following institutions provided invaluable information, resources, and/or experiences: the Arizona Chapter of the Japanese American Citizens League, Special Collections at the University of Arizona, the Bancroft Library at UC Berkeley, Densho, the Historical Museum at Fort Missoula, the Japanese American Museum of Oregon, the Japanese American Museum of San Jose, the Japanese American National Museum, the National Japanese American Historical Society, the National Park Service, the Topaz Museum, the Tucson Desert Art Museum, and the Tucson Jewish Museum and Holocaust Center.

In addition to the people I quote from the questionnaire, many people appear throughout *The Afterlife* and/or were important to the process of researching and writing it. Thank you to everyone who shared their experience and perspective with me—in conversations (in person, on the phone, on video, in classrooms, at events, over meals), interviews, emails, and letters, especially: Joel Alpert, Erin Aoyama, Kiik

Araki-Kawaguchi, Don Mee Choi, Carolyn Sugiyama Classen, Dot Devota, Cathlin Goulding, Kimiko Guthrie, Masako Guthrie, Patrick Hayashi, Mitchell Higa, Patti Hirahara, Kiku Hughes, Satsuki Ina, Mike Ishii, Karen Ishizuka, Elizabeth Ito, Yoshiko Kanazawa, traci kato-kiriyama, Emiko Katsumoto, Kiyoshi Katsumoto, Joni Kimoto, Aisuke Kondo, Koji Lau-Ozawa, Jami Nakamura Lin, Nikki Nojima Louis, Kirsten Emiko McAllister, Rei Magosaki, Mia Ayumi Malhotra, Kimiko Marr, Sean Miura, Linda Sachiko Morris, Heather Nagami, Suzy Nakamura, Tamiko Nimura, Chizu Omori, Emiko Omori, James Russell, Brynn Saito, Vince Schleitwiler, Christina Sharpe, Erin Shigaki, Patrick Shiroishi, Lauren Sumida, Rea Tajiri, Masako Takahashi, TT Takemoto, Kimiko Tanabe, Scott Tsuchitani, Nancy Ukai, Daryn Wakasa, Mitsuye Yamada, sho yamagushiku, and Karen Tei Yamashita.

Thank you to City Lights for supporting my work and giving me a history and a community to aspire towards in making it. Thank you to Stacey Lewis, for championing my work, and especially to Elaine Katzenberger, for believing in me, challenging me to think, clarifying my thinking, and helping me realize my dreams as a writer.

Thank you to the Shimoda and Yamashita families, especially Joy Endow, Sally Kerr, June Shimoda, Karen McAlister Shimoda, Kelly Shimoda, Midori Shimoda, Risa Shimoda, and Dean Yamashita.

And to Lisa and Yumi, for life.